T0208441

THE
TRANSONIC
SACRIFICE

THE TRANSONIC SACRIFICE

The Mystery of Death in Life

Glen C. Cutlip

Rev. date: 03/20/2020

To order additional copies of this book, contact:
Xlibris
1-888-795-4274
www.Xlibris.com
Orders@Xlibris.com
810503

CONTENTS

WORLD WITHOUT END

THE TRANSONIFIER

PREFACE

This Book as well as all other books and manuscripts, published or yet unpublished, written by the author, began after a dream experience in which I was encouraged to write. At that time, it didn't seem possible that I could do such a thing.

However, after other inner and outer experiences having taken place, the process of writing began. Although, at first, I wasn't sure of what I would be writing about, for the writings were somehow inspired.

One dream experience, of which one is not likely to forget, is the one where a being of an higher inner realm whispered in my ear, saying, "you are chosen." But what for? I wasn't sure at that time.

Another similar dream was one in which I was given the WORD to bring back. Again, at that time, I wasn't sure what that meant.

However, after several manuscripts were written and reread by me, things began to fit into place. That is, the dream experiences were becoming a reality.

Although the writings must speak for themselves, I feel now that I was chosen to present the *WORD,* the *WORD* of the Transonic Consciousness, which is the *WORD* embracing the realm of the end and the beginning of a cycle of time.

The Transonic *WORD*, then, is the *WORD* that takes in the harvesting of a previous cycle of time, and the *WORD* for the beginning of a new cycle of time.

Therefore, the *WORD* is the everlasting *WORD*, the everlasting gospel, as it were. Inasmuch as the *WORD* is the everlasting *WORD*, it is backed by an infinity of beings within the inner and outer realms of being.

CHAPTER ONE

Psychology of Death

We hear of the science, philosophy, and the psychology of life, but what about a science, a philosophy, a psychology of death?

We need to bring the hidden nature of death to light in order to see what it has to do with life. We get nowhere in life until we face what death might be.

It seems, for the most part, that religion is set apart as having no scientific, philosophical, or psychological importance. However, it seems we must go back to the scriptures to pick up the thread of understanding concerning this thing called death.

Both the Old and the New Testament give importance to the subject of death. Is not the overcoming of death said to be the final victory? How can one overcome death if one doesn't bother to find out what it is?

If death were what it appeared to be, it wouldn't seem to matter much that one chooses to ignore it. But death is not what it appears to be, and that is why the scriptures are ever seeking a means to bring the awareness of death to one's consciousness, to make it a part of one's consciousness. The awareness of death is just as important as the awareness of life.

Life and death move in cycles, reversing themselves, because death is not realized to be what it is. Many fear death for the same reason.

To think of death as simply a physical thing is to shut out the Light of what it might be. We need to get an overall picture of so-called death before we start making judgments as to what it might be. We need to sort out the seeming contradictions in what it is we consider it to be.

For example, consider the historical sacrifice of the Lamb of God. Is not the Lamb of God said to have been slain from before the foundation of the world? Thus, there must be more to it than a historical thing. It must be more than a physical thing.

For another example, what about the seeming contradiction in what St. Paul called the living sacrifice? There we seem to somehow have life and death locked into one another.

Thus, we must be living in death, yet that doesn't change the nature of death or life. It presents a different way of looking at both.

Another seeming contradiction is when Jesus spoke of the dead as hearing the voice of the Son of God and living. Thus, the dead spoken to and the dead that hear are the living-dead. Therefore, it must be more than just the body that is to experience death, for one experiences both death and the resurrection while living.

Death is something we are to experience in consciousness; otherwise, we cannot determine what it is.

As long as we don't know what death is, we tend to ignore or devise ways to escape it. Yet we sense that God doesn't seek to escape death.

Thus, we need to realize what God is in order to realize why it is that God gave the only begotten Son. We need to know what the Son is in order to realize why the Son gives all in sacrifice.

Of course, any kind of sacrifice will appear as something it is not to one seeing through the eyes of duality. Thus, one must, as it were, sacrifice sight in order to see what the sacrifice might be. That is, one must experience it that way.

If we give thought to the saying of Jesus that to lose one's life is to save it, we must conclude that there is more to both life and death than either appear to be. Life and death must somehow be cause and effect to the other's existence. Where would one be without the other?

Once we begin to realize that life and death exist only in relation to one another, we will be more than glad to welcome death as a Transonic part of our overall consciousness, for we will have begun to realize that death is a Transonic part of the nature of all things, from an atom to a universe.

How can we determine how it is that death may well be a part of the nature of all things? Again, we must determine what God is, and what the Son of God is.

Once we realize that God, to be God, must indeed be the All in All, which is to say that God must be the many in One, and the One in many. Thus, when God gave the only begotten Son for all, it was the One in many doing so. Thus, every atom, as it were, is represented in the giving of the only begotten Son. It is just that one is not necessarily aware of having done that. Becoming aware of having done that is the purpose of life, for we, as well as all things, participate in the giving whether it is realized or not.

Likewise, the only begotten Son is also the One in many and the many in One. Therefore, the Son of God represents all things from an atom to a universe. Thus, the sacrifice of the Son of God is made on your behalf as well as all things in the universe, for all things are represented in what the Son of God is.

Thus, all things are making the sacrifice whether it is realized or not. In other words, the Son of God, the Lord within you, is that which dwells in all things.

The One makes the sacrifice for the many, and the many make the sacrifice for the One. It's a universal, yet individual thing.

One may give another courage to make the sacrifice, but it is up to each to face up to what it is, since it is a part of one's Being in God.

Thus, there is no escape from what the sacrifice or death is. The escape is from what it appears to be. What death is, is not something we need to escape from, for the way out of it is into it, for that makes it a Transonic part of life.

The nature of the sacrifice is such that in the final conclusion, is never takes place. And that is because what it is, is not what it appears to be.

The sacrifice is a Transonic thing, which is to say it is, yet it is not a sacrifice. It cannot simply be a sacrifice, for it's something that is before the foundation of the world.

In other words, the sacrifice has neither beginning nor end; therefore, it has no time to take place in. It takes place in time without taking place in time, in that time has neither end nor beginning.

The substitute sacrifice is ever a part of the sacrifice to assure that the sacrifice is never really a sacrifice, and that death is never really death.

Thus, denying death doesn't make it go away, but losing life and finding it in death makes what it appears to be go away, for it disappears in life, and vice versa.

Accordingly, what death is in Transonic reality must be experienced in what appears as life, for life and death are transonically hidden one in the other; and are, therefore, transonically the same thing, which is to say that neither are what they appear to be. The one disappears in the other.

CHAPTER TWO

Transonic Death

Transonic terminology is used as a means of communicating that which cannot really be communicated. To say that something is Transonic is to say that it is a threefold seamless thing that is interchangeable within itself; and that the seamless parts come not together nor apart from one another, and that the parts and the whole are also interchangeable.

A Transonic thing represents that which is before and after itself, without being before and after itself, in that it is without beginning or end. A Transonic thing is that which begins without beginning, and ends without ending. The One Transonic thing is that which represents all things.

Accordingly, all things partake of the nature of the One Transonic thing. The nature of the One thing is as the nature of all things, and vice versa.

The Transonic thing is that which can be divided unto infinity, yet still represent the whole from which it was divided. The part cannot be separated from the whole. and vice versa.

Nothing can be done to a Transonic thing to change the nature of what it is. All things that appear to change are a part of the unchangeable Transon. The Transon changes without changing.

The Transon is indestructible, in that destruction is but a part of what it is. There is nothing that one could imagine that is not a Transonic part of Transon, for the Transon represents all things that are as well as all things that are not.

All things are represented in the Transon, for the unrepresented are represented there; for representation is a Transonic thing, and not what it appears to be.

All things are linked to the Transon, yet are not linked to it, for nothing comes together or apart from the Transon. Thus, all things are linked transonically.

The Transon represents the sacrificing of all things, for it is the one thing that has sacrificed all, including itself. It is what it is, and what it is not. Thus, it neither is nor is not.

The Transon transcends itself without doing it; therefore, what it is, is unknown to itself, for what it is, is also what it is not.

Accordingly, being and nonbeing are but a part of what the Transon is, for the Transon is that which is both being and nonbeing, yet neither, for it is also that which links being and nonbeing within itself into the threefold seamless consciousness, which links it to all things in and out of the universe.

Accordingly, Transonic death is linked to Transonic life, and Transonic losing is linked to Transonic finding. Therefore, dying is linked to living; therefore, losing life is finding it.

Thus, losing life in order to save it is not just a religious thing, for it represents the underlying nature of all things. It applies to all things whether realized or not. Losing and finding goes on at all levels of being from the so-called highest to the lowest.

One may experience death protonically (positively), electronically (negatively), neutronically (neutrally) until it is experienced transonically as it is in Transonic reality. Transonic death is realized to be Transonic life, and vice versa.

The Transonic Self cannot die, for it is as dead as it ever can be, for it is, as it were, the ever living sacrifice. It lives without living, and dies without dying, transcending both.

To be aware of death is to be unaware of it, in that the awareness causes it to disappear in Transonic life. It is in denying death that one gives it the illusion of being what it is not.

To lose life is to get it back, but not as it appeared to be before lost; that is, something apart from death. One gets life back reconciled with death, and that is much more than one could expect, for that represents the overcoming of death, the death that appeared to be.

In Transonic reality, to deny blindness, death, sin is to deny a part of one's Transonic reality, for in the All in All of Being, to deny anything is to deny a part of something of which all things are a Transonic part.

Thus, denying blindness is to, as it were, remain blind while seeming to see, for sight and blindness are transonically the same thing.

Denying deafness is to remain deaf while seeming to hear, for deafness and hearing are transonically the same thing.

Accordingly, denying anything is denying a part of an opposite that is a Transonic part of the denier of it.

Thus, death cannot be understood by the mind of duality, for it denies the right of death to be a Transonic part of life. Thus, it can be understood only by losing life and finding life and death to be transonically the same thing.

It is the interaction of life and death being the same thing that makes both to be transonically without end or beginning. The death of one thing and the birth of another is the birth and death of the same thing.

Accordingly, the one thing can be one thing and another thing to Transonic infinity, yet remain the one thing that it always is, the Transon, the ever unchanging changing One.

What lives, dies; what dies, lives. Thus, the Transon neither lives nor dies, for it does both without doing either. That which is not born does not die. The Transon is without beginning or end; therefore, the Transon is not born, and, therefore, does not die.

Thus, the Transon makes the sacrifice for all things, yet it does not make the sacrifice, for the Transon is ever the self-sacrificing one from before the foundation of anything. Accordingly, the Transon acts only in accord with what the nature of Transon is. Therefore, it sacrifices without doing it.

The nature of the sacrifice as well as the Transon is such that the sacrifice is ever being made moment by moment on behalf of all things, for it is the nature of the Transon to do that. The Transon doesn't make the sacrifice, for it is the sacrifice, and because the sacrifice is not a sacrifice. What it is, is a Transonic thing.

The nature of the Transon is as it is because that is the nature of that which is without beginning or end. As the Transon represents all things, all things represent the Transon.

Thus, all things are making the Transonic sacrifice whether realized or not, for all things partake of the nature of the Transon.

Accordingly, what Transon does for you is the same thing as what you do for Transon, even if you do so in unawareness.

As Transonic death is a Transonic part of the Transonic life of Transon, Transonic death is a transonic part of the Transonic life of all things.

CHAPTER THREE

Transonic Birth

As the Transonic sacrifice is before the foundation of the world, so is the Transonic birth from before the foundation of the world, for it is a Transonic part of the sacrifice.

Accordingly, Transonic death and Transonic life are both without beginning or end. Transonic birth and death are one hidden in the other as Transonic parts of the same thing.

We cannot understand life or death apart from one another; therefore, one must transcend duality before one can understand what life or death is.

However, one cannot consciously transcend duality without realizing what death is in Transonic reality. Before one can see beyond duality, which is seeing through the single eye, one must reconcile the seeming conflict of opposites.

Until opposites are reconciled through the core of being, one is blind while appearing to see, deaf, while appearing to hear, dead while appearing to live.

The realm of duality is the realm of the fall, the realm of the cycle of birth and death. Since birth and death are Transonic parts of the same thing, whether realized or not, one gets caught up in the cycle of birth and death.

That is, one gets trapped in the realm of duality until the lesson of duality is learned. The overcoming of death is the overcoming of duality, and vice versa.

To think that the birth of a thing is something that can be understood is to think in light of duality. One cannot understand birth because it transcends duality without doing it, for birth and death are transonically the same thing.

One cannot understand birth and death because the one is the Transonic reversal of the other. The understanding of birth is hidden in death, and vice versa.

The nature of a Transonic thing, which is the nature of all things, is not something that is supposed to be understood, for understanding is transonically transcended in Transonic understanding.

In Transonic understanding, one is to understand what is not to be understood. That is, one is to realize that what is not understood is a Transonic part of what is.

Moreover, to realize what is not understood, one must realize that what appears to be understood is not something that is understood, for understanding and misunderstanding are Transonic parts of the same thing.

Accordingly, what appears as knowledge is knowledge in part, for what appears as knowledge denies the ignorance that is a Transonic part of it. Knowledge in part is done away in Transonic knowledge.

To understand what is not understood is to understand without understanding, which is Transonic understanding.

To know what is not known is to know without knowing, which is to know that Transonic ignorance and Transonic knowledge are Transonic parts of the same thing.

To see what cannot be seen is to see without seeing, which is becoming blind in order to see, which produces Transonic seeing.

To be what cannot be is to be without being, which is to die and be born again, which is Transonic death and birth.

Thus, we need to bring the concept of being born again into the light of Transonic understanding. Being born again is not some narrow concept when seen through the single eye of being. That is, being born again is a Transonic part of that which is before the foundation of anything.

Being born again is not restricted to any one religion, nor is it something that is not a Transonic part of science, or any other branch of learning. It is a part of the Transonic nature of all things from an atom to a universe.

Dying and being born again is a process in both animate and inanimate things, for the process is a Transonic thing, which make the process a Transonic part of all things.

Thus, all things are in the process of becoming aware of what they are in Transonic reality. All things go through the process of birth and death, whether consciously or unconsciously until the lesson is learned.

That is, one is in the process of birth and death until one becomes conscious of being caught up in process. Then birth and death are realized to be Transonic servants of one another, and not what they appear to be.

The Transonic birth is the immaculate birth that is without spot or sin, for it takes place through the core of being where nothing defiled can enter.

The Transonic birth takes place not in the past or the future, for in Transonic reality, the past and the future are Transonic parts of the same thing.

However, the Transonic birth doesn't take place in the present to the exclusion of the past and the future, for the past, present, and the future are transonically the same place. It takes place in the Transonic present., for the Transonic present includes both the Transonic past and future.

The past, present, and the future are wedded seamlessly together in the Transonic consciousness. The Transonic present transcends itself, without doing it, for it is itself, yet not itself. It is the future, yet not the future. It is the past, yet not the past.

Thus, the Transonic present is that which is without beginning or end. It is in the Transonic present that the Transonic birth takes place. Therefore, the Transonic birth takes place without taking place, for birth and death are transonically the same thing, which is neither birth nor death.

Birth and death cannot take place, for there is no beginning for either to take place in. However, Transonic birth and death take place, for they take place in the context of that which is without beginning or end.

The Transonic birth and death are taking place everywhere simultaneously, for the process is without end or beginning. As Transonic birth and death are Transonic parts of the same thing, one must experience Transonic death in order to experience Transonic life. It is not something that another can do for you, for each must experience it individually. Then it is shared by all universally.

As life and death cannot be separated, to claim to be born again without realizing dying to be a part of it is to remain in the cycle of birth and death, just as to claim to see, denying blindness, is to remain blind.

To realize Transonic birth is to realize you are dead, yet alive, that you are an extension of yourself transonically.

CHAPTER FOUR

The Adventure of Life

Once life and death are taken out of their narrow context, and made to function as Transonic parts of one's consciousness, Transonic life takes in all things from before the foundation of the world. The adventure of life becomes more than one could ever have imagined while trapped in the mind of duality.

Transonic life, by means of Transonic death, is an extension of itself to Transonic infinity. So-called death is a means of moving from one body to another, or from one plane of being to another.

Accordingly, Transonic life is not limited to any body, or to any plane of being. The many mansions are there within one's being, within the all-in-one Transonic being.

Although Transonic life is without beginning or end, it is the only life there is. Transonic life is truly an adventure in that it is not bound to anything, including itself.

To be attached to life is to be bound to the cycle of birth and death. Life is the same as always. It's just that one is not attached to Transonic life, for attachment and detachment are Transonic parts of the same thing in Transonic life.

The adventure of life takes one beyond the confines of the worlds of bondage. To claim any one world to be the only world is to deny the many worlds or mansions within one's being in the all in all.

To be unattached to life is to be unattached to the world of one's dwelling. Thus, to be in the world, yet not in the world is the ideal mode of consciousness, for it takes in worlds within worlds to Transonic infinity, all within the One world without beginning or end.

We do things unconsciously until we learn to do them consciously, for the conscious and the unconscious are transonically the same thing.

We go into the inner mansions during the dream state, and experience things there, yet we may not be conscious of having done that. The adventure in that is in becoming aware of having done that.

Thus, the adventure really begins with the reconciliation of life and death, for one becomes transonically unattached to life, and is thereby prepared to experience out of body dream experiences consciously.

With life and death functioning as one thing, it seems a natural thing to move through the inner worlds of one's being.

Another's inner world experience may appear different from yours, but that's nothing to be concerned about, for your own experiences are so many, and so varied that they also appear different from one another. It's an adventure in there, yet experienced while out here, so to speak.

It's the Transonic self-sacrificing nature of the parts of one's threefold being that allows one to move through the inner worlds.

No sooner does a part of being die than it's born again, which is to say the Self dies without dying. With the overcoming of life and death comes the overcoming of spirit and matter; that is, spirit and matter are realized to be Transonic parts of the same thing.

With the overcoming of death, one is born of the Spirit. Thus, spirit and body become Transonic parts of the same thing. One's Transonic body is also a body of spirit. The spirit and matter bodies interchange positions as they moves through the inner worlds; that is, just as life and death interchange, without interchanging, in that the one is already transonically the other, spirit and matter interchange, without interchanging, for the one is also the other.

An ascending spirit world is an ascending matter world of a finer vibration. That is, when one gets to a spirit world, it becomes a matter world, for it was already that. The one performs the function of the other.

Thus, there is no profit in gaining the whole world if that means losing contact with the great adventure awaiting one in the inner worlds of interchanging spirit and matter. What's one world compared to the galaxies in there?

Thus, to be attached to anything, whether a world, a religion, or anything is to deny a part of being and to shut out the light of the inner worlds of being.

It's not that the world, or religion, or anything is bad within itself. It's the attachment to it that keeps the treasure hidden. The everlasting Kingdom of God is without beginning or end; therefore, it excludes nothing, yet allows things to seemingly exclude themselves.

However, those who exclude themselves from the Kingdom are still outside the Kingdom; therefore, they are still a Transonic part of the Kingdom, yet are not conscious of it, for the inside and the outside are transonically the same thing.

The Kingdom is inside and outside itself, without being either inside or outside, for the Kingdom is immanent, yet transcendent within itself.

In that the Kingdom is without beginning or end, there is nothing that is not somehow a Transonic part of it. Thus, to seek and find the Kingdom is to seek and find the one thing that includes all things in the universe of universes.

That is, finding the one thing that includes all things is to find the one Transonic thing, which is without beginning or end. The one Transonic thing contains the pattern of all things. Thus, the pattern of the everlasting sacrifice is seen to be a part of all things in the universe.

When the mind learns to function transonically in accord with the Transonic pattern, all seeming opposites conform to that pattern within the Transonic mind. All pairs of opposites are Transonic parts of one another, and are transonically linked to the Transonic mind of minds.

Any part of one's threefold, seamless being can function as the other part, for each part is transonically the other part. Each part is the other part, yet each part is a multiple of itself to Transonic infinity, which is the Transonic linkage of all thing in the universe.

Thus, every seeming opposite in the universe is a Transonic thing, and not what it appears to be.

The atoms of being conform to the mind that conceives them. The atoms of being conform to the Transonic pattern within the Transonic mind.

The adventure of Transonic life is an everlasting one, an everlasting journey. One may attain goals forever, for there is no end to such things. However, there is no everlasting satisfaction in any one attained goal, for the goal ever transcends itself.

The Transonic goal is the goal of goals, for it transcends itself as a part of the goal. Attaining fleeting goals is the concern of one trapped in the realm of duality, where the adventure is also fleeting.

CHAPTER FIVE

The Keys of Hell and Death

It is the one slain from before the foundation of the world that has the keys of hell and death. As the lamb that is slain from before the foundation of the world represents the all in all of being, the lamb represents the one in many and the many in one.

Thus, the keys of hell and death are received by the one who has identified with the lamb of God, and with the Transonic sacrifice of the lamb of God. That is, the one who sees the Son of God as the Son of God is becomes like unto the Son of God, and like unto the Transonic sacrifice.

The keys of hell and death go to the overcomer of hell and death, unto the one who realizes the Transonic sacrifice to be a Transonic part of one's being in God.

To have the keys of hell and death is to have the keys of the everlasting Kingdom, and of the everlasting gospel.

The overcomer of death has the keys of heaven and hell. Heaven and hell represent heaven and earth in that the one represents the seeming opposite of the other.

As opposites are Transonic parts of the same thing, heaven and earth are not separate from one another. Heaven and earth appear separate because of the scales, as it were, over the eyes of the one seeing through the eyes of duality.

Heaven and earth are not separate because both are a Transonic part of the Transonic sacrifice. That is, heaven and earth are sacrificed one for the other, which allows them to interchange positions.

However, the mind of duality does not know that heaven and earth are not separate places. Therefore, the one trapped in duality cycles back and forth from earth to heaven. Accordingly, heaven and earth are united whether realized or not.

To break the cycle of birth and death within duality, one must become the living sacrifice, as it were, thereby reconciling life and death.

Heaven above and earth (hell, death) below are transonically united, and cannot be separated. Heaven and hell (earth, death) occupy the realm of duality. The inner and outer realms of duality represent heaven and hell (earth, death). The one bound to duality moves back and forth without knowing such is taking place.

The overcomer of death has, as it were, earned the right to consciously move back and forth through these realms, mansions of being, finding pasture, as it were.

The overcomers of death have linked heaven and earth through the core of being, making the parts and that which links them a threefold seamless consciousness, which breaks the cycle of birth and death.

Heaven and earth are forever linked from before the foundation of either. That is, they were linked before they began, which is to say they have neither beginning nor end.

Accordingly, without beginning or end, one moves within the realm of duality (heaven and earth) unconsciously until the realm of duality is overcome through the Transonic sacrifice.

The problem of telling one that the realm of duality is the realm of hell and death is that one doesn't realize how that might be. Thus, the one trapped in duality ever needs the aid of a deliverer to show the way out of duality into the everlasting Kingdom of God.

The one trapped in duality doesn't realize there is infinitely more to be realized beyond the realm of duality. Moreover, such a one doesn't realize that to go beyond duality is to return to it, and thereby seeing it as it is, not just as it appears to be.

Therefore, losing duality is finding it plus what is beyond it. There is no such thing as giving apart from receiving.

As the overcomers of death has taken the sting, as it were, out of death, the sting is also taken out of hell. Thus, the one that can dwell in both heaven and hell has united the to, making one the counterpart of the other.

Thus, heaven and earth are rolled away, as it were, for they are not what they appear to be. The new heaven and the new earth are transonically the same thing, united transonically.

The Transonic heaven and earth reflect the consciousness of the Transonic sacrifice. Transonic heaven and earth is the realm of the threefold seamless Consciousness of the living Christ Self, where all things have been reconciled and delivered unto God, the all in all.

The threefold seamless Consciousness does not deny anything, for it is the Transonic reconciliation of all things. Thus, the threefold Christ Consciousness does not deny the Transonic sacrifice, for it is that.

It is through the living Christ Self at the core of being that the conflict of opposites is reconciled, transmuted, purified, and delivered unto God spotless.

Until opposites within one's being are reconciled, one is bound to the cycle of birth and death. As always, what is bound on earth is bound in heaven, for heaven and earth are transonically the same thing.

In order to attain liberation in heaven, one must attain it on earth. The mind of duality projects things to the future (that never arrives) things that must be taken care of in the now of Transonic time.

The threefold Christ Consciousness projects nothing away, for it weds all things together transonically. The now of Transonic time is omnipresent in the Christ Consciousness.

The Christ Consciousness represents the first and the last of all things, for it is without beginning or end. Anything without beginning or end represents the Christ Consciousness.

Anything, or anyone that sees the Christ as is becomes like unto the Christ, for one was already like unto the Christ unconsciously, for all things are without beginning or end whether' realized or not.

The revelation of that which is without beginning or end is the Everlasting Gospel, for there is nothing before or after that.

CHAPTER SIX

The Key of Knowledge

What was spoken nearly two thousand years ago concerning the key of knowledge is as fitting today as it was then. Here are the words of Jesus found in Luke 11:52:

"Woe unto you, lawyers! for ye have taken away the key of knowledge: ye entered not in yourselves, and them that were entering in ye hindered."

The above words are about as harsh as any can get unto those who would hinder one from entering the Kingdom of God. Yet those words were spoken with the greatest of love.

The lawyers are the ones who seek, whether conscious or unconsciously, to keep the conflict of opposites alive and well. They seek to keep the wolf and lamb of being from dwelling together in harmony.

The nature of entering the Kingdom is already complicated or hindering enough without others seeking to hinder one from entering it.

To enter the Kingdom, one must escape the bondage of duality, and that's not an easy thing to do, for one doesn't know that one is trapped. Thus, if one is not reminded of it, how is one to know?

By the very nature of one's being in God, it is the duty of one who knows of the bondage of duality to remind those who do not know.

Those who do not know of the bondage of duality are dependent on those who do know to give them assistance, for this is also a Transonic interaction.

The rescuer and the rescued are transonically the same thing. That is, the one comes to be or reverses to the other. Such is the process of Transonic creation, and is without beginning or end.

Thus, the one in position to rescue another has been in the position of needing to be rescued, and may well be in that position again.

When one rescues another from the bondage of duality, the other is in position to rescue another. Such is the Transonic perfection built into the Transonic creation.

Thus, the rescue mission on behalf of all trapped in duality is a mission without beginning or end just as the Kingdom is.

Accordingly, we are all Transonic co-workers in the all in all of being, for that's the way it's always been, is, and shall be, for that's the nature of that which is without beginning or end. Thus, they who would hinder one from the everlasting Kingdom do so to their own detriment, for it goes contrary to the nature of one's creation in God.

Although it's not easy to escape the bondage of duality, in that it requires the Transonic sacrifice, it is well worth the sacrifice. Thus, it's not easy to get one trapped in duality to realize such is the case.

To escape duality is to sacrifice all, give all, which is to receive all. But the dual mind doesn't know that, so it appears that to lose duality is to lose all and that's it.

Thus, one tends to hold on to duality until the situation in life takes one to the point where the conflicts of duality appear to leave one with no other choice.

Accordingly, the conflicts of duality have a way of correcting themselves, for duality will destroy itself by means of the conflict within itself if it doesn't realize the Transonic sacrifice, and thereby destroy itself transonically, which is to make it indestructible, for Transonic destruction is not destruction as it would appear to the dual mind; for Transonic destruction is also Transonic creation.

That is, giving up, losing, destroying, or sacrificing duality is the means of getting it back reconciled unto the threefold Christ Consciousness.

Instead of losing, one gains all by losing duality, for losing is but finding. Thus, they who are intent on holding on to duality, and encouraging others to do so will find the conclusion to be self-destruction.

Thus, one way or the other one faces the Transonic sacrifice, for there is no escaping it, in that it is a Transonic part of one's creation in the all in all of being.

That is, all the wealth, fame, power, or name that one acquires while in the bondage of duality comes to nothing, for it denies the Transonic reality of being that is without beginning or end.

With the age of the reconciliation of all things through Christ unto God of the threefold reconciled Consciousness, those who seem to have are seen to have nothing, for what is built on duality is as on sinking sand. It is the works of duality that is the wood, hay, and stubble, as it were, that is burned away.

The Truth of being that endures the flaming fire of the Christ Consciousness is the Truth that is without beginning or end.

Although the reconciliation of all things unto God through the Christ of being transcends wealth, fame, power, and name, such things are still there transferred to the age of the reconciliation.

Thus, the first become the last and the last become the first as the reversal takes place. Those who may become trapped in the age of the reconciliation will have the assistance of those who are not trapped, for the new creation is out of the old, and goes on as though it never took place for creation is without beginning or end.

Although the realm of duality is not what it appears to be, it is a transonically omnipresent thing. Therefore, at one level of being or the other anywhere in creation is the potential of becoming trapped in the conflict of duality.

Accordingly, the solution to that must be built into the creation before the creation takes place. That is, when one gets trapped in duality, it should be remembered that, as always, salvation is ever at the door, the core, the Christ Self of one's being in God. Salvation is ever the balancing of opposites within one's being. Salvation is ever a Transonic thing, which is without beginning or end.

Thus, if one were to leave a message that would be everlastingly handed down., one would want that message to contain the means of reconciling the opposites within one's being.

That is, if one were to leave a message, and say a million years or so later one were to become trapped in duality, one would want such a message to be there.

However, that's the nature of an everlasting message in the first place. The message is ever there, for it is without beginning or end, and, therefore, transonically omnipresent.

It's the written or spoken message that tends to get distorted. It's the written or spoken Word that needs to be preserved as pure as possible, for the written Word is that which connects one to the unwritten Word. The written and the unwritten Word are transonically the same thing. Thus, both are ever preserved together.

The key of knowledge needs to be preserved in the written Word, and available to all who seek that knowledge, for the one who would withhold it also needs access to that knowledge.

The one who would withhold the key of knowledge from another will have it withheld from him or her when needed, for doing unto another is doing unto yourself, for all are transonically linked together in the Transonic Consciousness of the living Christ of one's being unto God, the all in all.

CHAPTER SEVEN

The Transonic Sacrifice

Once we realize that the Transonic sacrifice is without beginning or end, and that it is a Transonic part of all things in creation, we can realize how that all things are transonically united through the Transonic sacrifice.

All of creation partakes of the salvation through the Transonic sacrifice, for all of creation is a Transonic part of the Transonic sacrifice. All the atoms of creation are ever dying without dying; for within all creation, the Transonic sacrifice is also the Transonic substitute sacrifice.

Thus, all things are participating in the Transonic sacrifice either consciously or unconsciously. The Transonic sacrifice is the same throughout the mineral, plant, animal, and human Kingdoms, and all beyond that.

The Transonic sacrifice is what assures that for every death there is a birth, that to die is to be born again. It is the forms that the Transonic Christ Consciousness dwells in that die. It's the forms that change within the unchangeable. Throughout the changing of forms, the Christ Consciousness remains unchanged.

That is, the One Transonic Consciousness is the One Consciousness of all forms, for it is the Consciousness of all. There is no consciousness that is not the Transonic Consciousness, for the Transonic Consciousness is that which is without beginning or end. There can be no other, nor need there be.

The one thing that is all things can take on forms to Transonic infinity, yet remain what it is, that which is both form and formlessness reconciled.

For example, take fuel such as wood. We know there is the form of fire in the form of wood, for we can see it coming out.

That is, when the fuel is sacrificing itself as fuel, the form changes to fire, yet the consciousness of the forms remain the same, for both forms are a Transonic part of the one consciousness.

Thus, any form is a threefold form that interchanges within itself within the one form. When the threefold form is transcended, the threefold form changes to another form. One form represents another to Transonic infinity, for by means of the Transonic sacrifice, one form can become another, for it is transonically the one form in many, and the many in one.

Thus, all forms are transonically united to the one body of God, the all in all. To do unto anything is to do unto God, for there is nothing excluded from God.

All things that appear to begin and end do so in the context of that which is without beginning or end, the Transonic Christ Consciousness.

Just as physical forms change within the one form, we see the same thing in relation to past, present, and future, which appear abstract. The abstract forms of past, present, and future are interchangeable, yet the consciousness of them is the same, for the threefold abstract forms are transonically the same form.

That is, what appears as the future takes on the form of the present., and then the form of the past. The future is all three forms in one form. The future is a self-sacrificing form.

The present gives way to the future and also to the past. The present is three forms in one form. The present is a self-sacrificing form.

The past was the future, and then the present before it become the past. The past is three forms in one form. It also is a self-sacrificing form. The past, present, and the future are transonically the same thing.

By means of the Transonic sacrifice within the past, present, and the future, they are a trinity that is a multiple of itself to Transonic infinity. That is, one part of the trinity is ever dying for the other, and becoming the other. Thus, the unchangeable past, present, and future are ever changing without changing. Nothing remains the same, yet nothing changes.

The past, present, and the future are transonically linked to all things in the universe, for they are of the Transonic Consciousness, which is without beginning or end. The past, present, and the future, being the same thing, there isn't anywhere for one to end and the other to begin.

Anything one can see, or anything one can think of is of the nature of the Transonic Consciousness. All things conform to the threefold interchange that is a multiple of itself to Transonic infinity.

Thinking is a threefold interchange within itself. Thus, to think transonically is to think without thinking. Dual mind thinking is thinking in part, just as dual mind knowledge is knowledge in part.

The mind of Christ transcends both the mind and the knowledge of duality without doing it, in that the mind of Christ is the reconciliation of all things within itself.

The mind of Christ is the Transonic reconciliation of all things in the universe. The Christ is that which dwells within all things as that thing is in Transonic reality.

Thus, by means of the Transonic sacrifice of the Christ Consciousness from before the foundation of the world, all things are reconciled unto God. By means of the sacrifice, all things are one with God whether realized or not.

To be one with God is to be one with all things in the universe, from the lowest to the highest. Thus, to say you love God to the exclusion of something else is to deny what God is, for there is none else other than God, the all in all.

Thus, one is one with the seemingly lower forms of life as well as the higher forms. One is one with the lower forms, in that one has progressed through those forms. One is not necessarily conscious of having been in the lover forms because the consciousness within them remains the same, and because of the unconscious factor involved.

That is, one doesn't remember the cycle of birth and death. When one becomes aware of the birth and death cycle, one is a conscious overcomer of death. It is then that one becomes more attuned to nature, and to the many forms of which one has ever been a Transonic part.

CHAPTER EIGHT

The Living Sacrifice

Once we realize the nature of the Transonic sacrifice, the concept of the living sacrifice takes on new meaning. That is, we come to understand that presenting the body a living sacrifice is not just an optional thing, for one's body is a living sacrifice whether one realizes it or not.

The body dies and takes on another form whether one is conscious of the process or not. Thus, one is both dead and alive at the same time while in the body, for life and death are transonically the same thing.

By becoming aware of the Transonic sacrifice of the ever living Christ of one's being, and becoming that sacrifice, one becomes the living sacrifice. Life and death become transonically the same thing within one's consciousness.

One comes to realize that one is not bound to any one form, for one identifies with the formless form of the living Christ of one's being.

By presenting the body a living sacrifice, one is no longer attached to the body, or to life or death. By presenting the body a living sacrifice, one is reconciling life and death, which breaks the cycle of birth and death in present consciousness.

By living in death, one overcomes death. By reconciling life and death, one overcomes duality. Reconciling life and death is reconciling the opposites of one's being unto the threefold, sacrificing Christ Consciousness.

By living in death, there is no death to look forward to, in that one has already put it in the present, the, past, and the future.

By living in death, one is living in accord with that which is without beginning or end. Life and death are transonically the same thing; therefore, they cannot be separated or brought together. There is no place for either to end or begin.

Living in death is living in the Transonic knowledge that there is no death as it would appear to be. Living in death eliminates the consciousness of death, for death is overcome in life.

By living in the consciousness of the living sacrifice, one prepares the consciousness to transfer from one form to another without losing consciousness in the process, for one realizes that one is not just any one form.

Until one adjusts to the concept of changing forms, one may well be confused when, in an inner world, the consciousness of an outer form appears there in a different form. That is, in the inner world, one may appear in what appears as a past form, or what appears as a future form, and not knowing how that might be, may get confused by it.

Thus, consciousness must adjust to the changing of form in order to be at home, as it were, in any form on a temporary basis.

By living in the consciousness of the sacrificing of the body, one is transonically becoming detached from the bondage to any one form.

Thus, to establish an identity from one form to another, one must identify with the formless form of the living Christ Consciousness, which is the essence of what you are in Transonic reality.

The formless form is the form that can, as it were, move through both spirit and matter, for the formless form is both spirit and matter reconciled. It is the consciousness of the formless form that moves interdimensionally through the planes of being.

By becoming conscious of a particular form, one becomes temporarily bound to it. While moving in the formless form, one is no more conscious of the form than of the formless, and thereby moves through matter as through it were really not matter. The form and the formless parts of one's being are self-sacrificing. The one dies and becomes the other simultaneously.

It is one thing to seek to acquire things selfishly, ignoring the Transonic sacrifice, and another thing to acquire things by way of sacrificing all things.

The things acquired selfishly are not permanent, and therefore pass away in time. They appear attractive for the time being, but are fleeting.

That which is acquired through giving doesn't ignore the Transonic sacrifice, for giving and receiving are thereby realized to be the same thing.

By recognizing the Transonic sacrifice in the nature of all things, what one acquires is permanent, in that it is based on that which is without beginning or end.

To have apart from not having is seeming to have. That is why such things pass away. To truly have one must give up having, and thereby have without having, for then nothing can pass away, for it had already passed away, yet remained.

The things acquired in the context of duality deny the Transonic sacrifice in the nature of creation. Thus, claiming to have something is to deny that one also has nothing. Claiming to have denies one the right to have anything that endures to everlasting.

By having nothing, one has all things, for all things and nothing are transonically the same thing.

With an infinite number of things to have, there is no point in trying to have all at the same time. Thus, one must learn to have without having, and thereby appear to have something, knowing all the while that one doesn't really possess it, for it passes away.

Thus, by having without having, one allows them to interchange, just as all things interchange within the Transonic Consciousness.

Just as one's form changes to another, what one has changes to having something else to Transonic infinity. By giving up having a certain thing, one comes to have something else. Having and not having are transonically the same thing.

Thus, the true riches are beyond what the dual mind can conceive. It is just that the dual mind tends to be ever hardened against itself. Thus, until the dual mind realizes, through experience, that things are, indeed, fleeting, there is not much one can do to convince it otherwise.

Who is to say that the one who has all the means to live a complicated life is any better off than one who content to live a simple life?

However, what we are really reaching for is the reconciliation of the complex and the simple life, not just one or the other. The complex and the simple life is the same life viewed differently.

CHAPTER NINE

The Transonic Reconciliation

With an understanding of the universality of the Transonic sacrifice of Christ, the Lamb of God, from before the foundation of the world, we come to realize how it is that all things are gathered unto the Christ, and delivered unto God that God may be all in all.

For it is now altogether in the realm of the possibility of being an accomplished fact. Let us review the word of St. Paul concerning this in Ephesians 1:10: "That in the dispensation of the fullness of times he might gather together in one all things in Christ both which are in heaven, and which are on earth; even in him."

Again in I Corinthians 15:22-28 we read: "For in Adam all die, even so in Christ shall all be made alive. But, every man in his own order: Christ the firstfruits: afterwards they that are Christ's at his coming. Then cometh the end, when he shall have delivered up the kingdom to God, even the Father; when he shall have put down all. rule and authority and power. For he must reign, till he hath put all enemies under his feet. The last enemy that shall be destroyed is death. For he hath put all things under his feet. But when he saith all things are but under him, it is manifest that he is excepted, which did put all things him. And when all things shall be subdued unto him, then shall the Son also himself be subject unto him that put all things under him, that God may be all in all."

As we have now realized, the Transonic sacrifice is without beginning or end. Therefore, the Transonic sacrifice has ever been an accomplished fact of nature. It is just that it takes the awareness of that to fulfill the purpose of it.

Thus, all the historical teachings concerning the sacrifice is the means of bringing the awareness of the sacrifice to the consciousness of all, so that all may experience the consciousness of it.

The Christ that is without beginning or end is the everlasting sacrifice. The historical Christ is the means of bringing the awareness of the everlasting Christ to the awareness of all.

Thus, to identify with the historical Christ is to eventually identify with the everlasting Christ, which is to identify with both the historical and the everlasting sacrifice.

One comes to identify with the everlasting sacrifice of the Christ when one comes to see the Christ as is, for then one realizes that one is, and has always been like unto the Christ. It was, and is a matter of realizing what already is an accomplished fact in the mind of God.

As the Christ is without beginning or end, the Christ represents all that was, is, or shall be. Thus, to gather all things unto and under the feet of Christ is to gather all things unto and under the Transonic reality of what they are, have been, and shall be.

As the last enemy to be destroyed is death, the awareness of the Transonic sacrifice makes that an accomplished fact of one's being in God.

The Christ is that which dwells in all things, thereby representing all things. The Christ is not something apart from you. To do unto another is to do unto Christ. To do unto Christ is to do unto you.

Thus, as all things are gathered unto Christ, nothing is lost or taken away, for the Christ represents you and all things. As the Christ, representing all, delivers the Kingdom unto God, it is delivered on your behalf.

As to deliver or gather all things unto Christ is to deliver all things unto yourself, in that the Christ is a Transonic part, of you, as Christ delivers all unto God, it is unto the Christ of all, for the Christ is one with God, the all in all.

Thus, the all in all of God is not something apart from anything. To deliver the Kingdom unto God is to deliver it unto all in God. Thus, the delivering or the giving up of the Kingdom unto God is not what it might appear to be, for the giving up of it is the receiving of it. The giving up and the receiving are transonically the same thing.

Just as the Transonic sacrifice was ever there awaiting awareness, the Kingdom has ever been delivered unto God. It's a matter of awaking to that Transonic fact.

The process of delivering the Kingdom unto God is the means of bringing the nature of the Kingdom to one's awareness. To find the Kingdom is to find that which allows all things to be added unto you.

The Kingdom is, and has ever been without beginning or end. Everything within the Kingdom is an interaction of a threefold thing multiplied to Transonic infinity.

By means of such interaction, what is turned over to God is returned to you, for that's the nature of all things from before the foundation of the world.

Thus, the nature of God is as the nature of all. things. The Transonic sacrifice is not something apart from God, for God is that. God receives the Kingdom without receiving it. Thus, the Kingdom is where it was, is, and ever shall be, transonically omnipresent throughout the Transonic universe of universes.

Thus, the reconciliation of all things unto God is a Transonic reconciliation. That is, things are ever reconciled in the mind of God. It's a matter of becoming aware of that Transonic fact.

To turn everything one could possibly imagine having over to God is to receive it back. It is just that when one receives it back, one has it without having it. That is, one is no longer attached to what one has.

Thus, one comes to realize that Christ and God are transonically the same being. One comes to realize that everything, from an atom to a universe, is a Transonic thing, and that one thing represents all things.

One comes to realize that one is a Transonic being; and, therefore, cannot claim to have anything, for having and not having are transonically the same thing. To have is not to have, and not to have is to have.

Thus, in the all in all of God, all things are moment by moment being returned back, which is the interaction of giving and receiving.

Everything is transonically transcended in the Transonic Consciousness, and that is what makes the creation of God transonically perfect, regardless of what it appears to be.

To be attached to something is to be attached to the pain of having it taken away. Of course, experience teaches that. If nature didn't provide for the passing away of attachments, things would only become a clutter. To have without having is the ideal mode of consciousness.

The concept of having without having is more clearly seen as a practical thing from within the inner worlds. That is, when one needs transportation, it can appear for the purpose of the occasion, and then disappear; and, therefore, not clutter up anything. That is perfection that staggers the imagination.

Thus, in the context of having without having, as seen from the inner worlds, one has access to an infinite number of things, but only uses what is suited for the occasion. Thus, materializing and dematerializing are seen to be Transonic parts of the same thing. Thus, the Transonic sacrifice is seen to be a Transonic part all things that are transonically reconciled through the Christ of one's being unto God, the all in all of being.

CHAPTER TEN

The Selfless Self

By means of the completed cycle of the Transonic sacrifice, we realize that God has transonically sacrificed all for creation, and that creation has transonically sacrificed all for God. That is, as all things are delivered through Christ unto God, the cycle is completed, and God is realized to be the all in all of Being.

Through the interaction of the Transonic sacrifice, God and you are reconciled. God and you are seen as one hidden in the other as the other. There is nothing that can separate one from God, for God, man and woman are transonically indivisible.

Thus, the Kingdom that is delivered through Christ unto God is returned to the creation, for God and the creation of God are working together in the everlasting Kingdom.

What is required of God is what is required of the creation of God. What God does for you, you do for God, either consciously or unconsciously. By delivering all back to God, one becomes conscious of the interaction of God and the creation of God.

That is, God, man, and woman come to function within the Transonic Christ Consciousness of God and the creation of God. All things were functioning within the Transonic mind of Christ, but until one returns all back to God, the mind of Christ is not seen as it is in Transonic reality.

The mind of Christ is the mind of God and the mind of you. The mind of Christ is the one mind that is the mind of all things.

To see the mind of Christ as it is, is to see that mind as your mind, yet the mind of Christ. That is, the mind of Christ is shared by all. One cannot possess the mind of Christ as through it were one's own, for the mind of Christ is an interaction of giving and receiving within itself.

The mind of Christ is not limited to any one thing, or to any one level of functioning. It is the interchangeability of the mind within itself to Transonic infinity that allows it to be what it is in Transonic reality.

Just as there are forms within forms to Transonic infinity within the one form, there are minds within minds to Transonic infinity within the one Transonic mind of Christ.

As the one mind can function within all forms, the mind is not attached to itself. Thus, it can appear to be attached to a particular form, and later appear to be detached from it, and thereby appear to become attached to another form, and so on to Transonic infinity.

Thus, the mind and the body are transonically linked together without being linked together. That is, mind and body both transcend themselves without doing it to Transonic infinity.

Therefore, the sacrificing mind gets itself back, for it is ever a Transonic part of all things. The sacrifice and the substitute sacrifice are transonically the same thing. This is realized with the completed cycle of the Transonic sacrifice.

As both God and the creation of God interact, both are giving and receiving from one another. Thus, the two-way sacrifice cancels the sacrifice. That is, the sacrifice and the substitute sacrifice cancel one another.

As the Christ of God and God are revealed to be the Transonic part and the Transonic whole of creation, what one does unto God is done unto oneself. That is, the Christ and God are revealed to be a Transonic extension of one's self in God.

Thus, the sacrificing of anything unto God is sacrificing it to another part of your being in God, for God is not something separate from you.

The mind of God is the Transonic mind of you. The Transonic mind is separate from itself without being separate, which allows for the Transonic transfer of itself interdimensionally.

It is by delivering all things back to God through the Christ that makes things spotless before God. That is, what returns to God through the Christ Self of one's being goes through the neutronic core of one's being, and that is where the purification takes place.

Thus, what is delivered unto God through the Christ is returned purified. To give one's life through Christ unto God is to have life and death purified in the core, the fire of being, and returned transonically purified.

Therefore, it is realized that the Christ is a flaming fire of judgment on the one hand, and the means of presenting one spotless before God on the other.

That is, by resisting the everlasting, Transonic sacrifice, one brings the destruction of the fire of being, which is nature's way, which is Gods way of purifying things.

That is, what is not built upon the foundation that is without beginning or end, becomes., as it were, wood, hay, and stubble; and such is what is burned away in the fire of the living Christ of one's being in God.

Although the nature of God changes not, one tends to think it might, and thus ignores the Transonic fact that there is ever something in the nature of God that exacts justice.

That is, God is fearful, in that God is a part of you. Thus, what one does unto God comes under the law of cause and effect, and therefore comes back to one.

Therefore, it's not just that God is a fearful being, but that you are a fearful being unto yourself. That is, you are a fearful being unto yourself until you reconcile the fear and the love through the Christ unto God, which is ever a Transonic part of you.

Thus, when it is all said and done, one cannot blame God for anything, for one will become aware of what one has done with the talents received from God.

One way or the other, one comes to realize that there is no place to escape or hide from God, for God is revealed to be a Transonic part of all things.

One comes to realize that one has ever been functioning in the mind of God at one level or the other, and that one is still functioning in the mind of God.

To return all that has been received from God back to God is to realize that the self of God is a selfless self. The self of God is the self of all things, and is, therefore, not bound to itself.

The self of God and the self of all things is the same Transonic self, The self of selves is the selfless self. The self of God and the self of the people of God is a threefold self that is a multiple of itself to Transonic infinity.

The self of God and the self of you become or are realized to be the same Transonic self.

Accordingly, with the completed cycle of the Transonic sacrifice, it is realized how that God and the people of God walk together, for nothing is impossible with God. The seemingly impossible is made possible, for possibility and impossibility are realized to be transonically the same thing.

CHAPTER ELEVEN

The Temple of God

By delivering all things unto God through the Christ of one's being in God, one realizes how it is that God does, indeed, walk with the people of God. By delivering all unto God, it is realized that the body is the temple of God. By acting on faith that the body is the temple of God, one eventually realizes the Transonic fact of it.

One comes to realize that God dwells within one's body temple, which is the temple of God. The body of God and you, and of all things, are purchased by means of the Transonic sacrifice.

Thus, as one realizes that one is that Transonic sacrifice, one realizes that one has paid the price for the redemption of the body. The body is redeemed through the Transonic sacrifice of one's being in God. In that the sacrifice is one without being one, the body is redeemed without being redeemed.

The sacrifice is not a sacrifice, for it also the substitute sacrifice. The one is hidden in the other. Therefore, the body is redeemed, in that another body becomes the substitute or replacement for the one that passes away.

By means of the interaction of the sacrifice and the substitute sacrifice, one is the body, yet not the body, for one is a body within a body to Transonic infinity.

Inasmuch as one pays the price without paying it, in that the substitute sacrifice is a part of the sacrifice, it is as though one pays the price, yet another does it.

The nature of one's being in God is such that it appears that another does what one does, for the nature of one's being in God is such that one is an extension of oneself to Transonic infinity.

What one does in the being of God, one does in accord with the being of God, for there is none else other than God. Just as God transcends God in order to be all things in creation, one transcends oneself in order to be what one is in God.

As one transcends the self in God, one transcends the body in God. Thus, one does not own the body, for one owns it without owning it, for it is an extension of itself to Transonic infinity.

Thus, by surrendering the body to God, there is always a body provided for the one passing away, for the body that is provided is an inner body of the outer body. The Transonic reason for not identifying with a particular body is that one is ever more than any one body. Your body is God's and not yours in the sense that your body is yours, yet not yours; for the body is the body of God, and you. God and you are one hidden in the other until brought to light in the Christ Consciousness.

Thus, one cannot claim to own the body, for God does not claim to own it, for God gives all that is received. As to give is to receive, to disown the body is to own it, for the body is not what it appears to be, in that it is a body within a body to Transonic infinity.

By allowing the body to be delivered unto God through the living Christ self, one receives it back as the dwelling place, the temple of God.

The body has ever been the temple of God. The glory of that is taken away by ignoring the Christ at the core of being. As in all things, it is a matter of becoming aware of the original, Transonic glory, which appears lost in duality.

By delivering the mind unto God through Christ, one receives it back as the purified mind of God. Thus, what is delivered unto God comes back purified, for it goes through the purifying fire at the core of one's being in God.

The Christ of one's being, as the mediator, has ever been delivering all things unto God on your behalf. Thus, one faces the destruction of bodies within bodies in unawareness until one is prepared to face it in awareness.

By becoming aware that the destruction must take place, in that it is a Transonic part of one's being in God, one enters the Christ Consciousness and allows the Christ to deliver the creation and the destruction unto God, and thus gets the creation back reconciled with the destruction.

Thus, one enters the destruction of the self and returns from it in conscious awareness that creation and destruction are transonically the same thing.

By delivering all things unto God through Christ, one is delivering the entire realm of duality unto God, and receiving it back purified. Thus, the Christ Consciousness is beyond the duality of life and death, in that it is the reconciliation of life and death. Life and death are transonically the same thing in the Christ Consciousness.

The Christ Consciousness is a threefold oneness that transcends that oneness within that threefold oneness, yet it is a multiple of that threefold oneness to Transonic infinity.

Although the Christ Consciousness may appear light years from the consciousness of duality, it is the logical outcome of reconciling the opposites of duality.

Those who have been looking for the appearing of the Christ Consciousness can now realize how it is that by seeing the Christ Consciousness as it is, one becomes like unto it, for it has ever been a Transonic part of one's consciousness, which became obscured in duality.

The light of the Christ Consciousness destroys the illusion of duality, burning away all that is impure within it.

The Christ Consciousness is a revelation of what you are and ever have been in the being of God. In that the Christ Consciousness is the reconciliation of duality, one enters the Christ Consciousness as a babe, as it were. That is, one is born into it.

Just as there was the process of becoming aware of what the Christ is in order to consciously enter it, there is the process of developing the Christ Consciousness. Everything from before the foundation of the world has been the process of developing an awareness of the Christ Consciousness, for it is without beginning or end.

The Christ Consciousness is not something that allows a simple explanation. It is complicated enough for the experienced to explain it to him or her, for it is neither simple nor complex. It is in seeing the one to the exclusion of the other that causes the confusion within mind that divides itself into the simple and the complex.

Thus, the Christ Consciousness cannot be completely explained to another, for one must be led to the experiencing of it; for then one begins the process of explaining it to oneself, and that is how one learns of that which transcends learning and teaching.

One is led to experience the Christ Consciousness.

That is, when one can see the Christ Consciousness in another, one is seeing it in oneself, for seeing the Christ as is, is to be like unto the Christ. By denying the Christ within another, one is denying it within oneself.

Thus, with the appearing of the Christ Consciousness, all have the opportunity of seeing the Christ as is, and thereby to become like unto the Christ.

Such is the manner of reaping the harvest, of gathering the elect from all who profess to know Christ.

Thus, the enduring unto the end is the enduring unto the appearing of the Christ Consciousness. Those who come to see the Christ Consciousness as it is become the elect of Christ.

The brightness of the Christ Consciousness destroys the man of sin, the man of duality. Thus, the appearing of the Christ Consciousness effects all.

That is, those who don't enter the Christ, the ark of being, as it were, are left, as it were, behind to endure what duality brings them. For one thing, there is the lost opportunity of forging an identity with the living Christ Consciousness of one's being in God.

It is the Christ Consciousness that lifts one out of the conflict of opposites within the realm of duality.

Within the Christ Consciousness, all things are being delivered unto God and returned moment by moment, for it is God delivering and returning all things unto God. Delivering and returning, giving and receiving are but an interaction within the being of God, for God, transcending all, dwells in the body temple of every man, woman, and child.

CHAPTER TWELVE

Cause and Effect

By developing the Christ Consciousness, we are developing a consciousness of unified oneness in the nature of all things, for the Christ Consciousness is the Transonic reconciliation of all things unto God.

Therefore, cause and effect are transonically the same thing in the Christ Consciousness. That is, there is neither cause nor effect apart from one another.

As cause and effect are delivered unto God through Christ, they are received back reconciled. Thus, cause and effect disappear one into the other.

In the Christ Consciousness, Transonic life is seen to be Transonic death. There is no separation one from the other, for the one is the cause and the effect of the other. To be born is to die, and to die is to be born again. Cause and effect are interchangeable parts of the same thing.

As birth and death are the cause and effect of one another, to overcome death is to overcome life, which is overcoming the cause and effect relationship of life and death.

One overcomes the cause and effect relationship by delivering the cause and effect relationship unto God through Christ, and having it returned transonically unified.

There is neither male nor female in the Christ Consciousness, in that the Christ Consciousness is the reconciliation of all opposites within itself. The positive and the negative of all things cancel one another without doing it.

That is, the positive and the negative cancel and replace themselves, for the one is already transonically the other to Transonic infinity.

It is the threefold interaction, of positive, negative, and, neutral, of the proton, electron, and neutron of consciousness that makes it impossible to say what anything is, for the one thing is all things, and all things are the one thing.

One cannot pen down the Christ Consciousness as to say it is any one thing, for all parts within the whole of creation within the Christ Consciousness are interchangeable with all other parts, and with all other wholes.

That is, any part of being can appear as any other part. Thus, to judge by appearances is to misjudge everything.

One cannot pen down the Christ Consciousness because the Christ Consciousness is without beginning or end. Since all things are within the Christ Consciousness, all things are transonically without beginning or end.

Thus, the threefold interaction of a threefold being within itself, multiplied to infinity, is the way things are, for that is the way of all things that are without beginning or end.

Thus, the Christ Consciousness is attached to all things without being attached to anything, for attachment and detachment are appearances within that which has neither beginning nor end.

By functioning within the consciousness that transcends itself without doing it, one is consciously functioning within the Christ Consciousness.

The Consciousness that ever reaches before and after itself is the Christ Consciousness. It is as though the Christ Consciousness has nowhere to be, for it transcends itself from before the foundation of the world.

It is just that the Christ Consciousness is not bound to be at any one place, for it can appear anywhere in the universe of universes. It is as though everywhere is the home of the Christ Consciousness, yet nowhere is.

It is just that the Christ Consciousness transcends time without doing it. It is everywhere, yet nowhere, at one point, yet all points transonically, for there is nothing excluded from the Christ Consciousness, for it is all that is, and all that is not, reconciled.

Thus, to function within the Christ Consciousness is to function within the reconciliation of all things, bringing cause and effect under the control of one's Christ Consciousness. That is, by delivering all unto God through Christ, the cycle of cause and effect, of birth and death is broken.

After delivering all things unto God and receiving the purified Christ Consciousness, one does all things unto God. Thereby, moment by moment the cause and effect of birth and death, of creating karma is transonically neutralized, for cause and effect become Transonic parts of the same thing.

Thus, by living in the Christ Consciousness of the reconciliation of all things unto God, one is not creating attachments to things that pass away and come to be again, such as life and death.

One cannot get control of consciousness until all is delivered unto God through the Christ of one's being in God.

To get control of consciousness within the being of God is to get control of it without getting control of it, for there, the control is transonically transcended.

Thus, to seek to control something is not to know what control is in Transonic reality. One gets control by relinquishing all control unto God, and receiving it as Transonic purified control.

By assuming that one can control something, one is assuming that control has an absolute meaning; and one, thereby, becomes attached to the limited control of things.

That is, while one is seeking and maintaining control over something, one is denying the other infinite number of things that could come under one's control. If one loses control over something because of the attachments to it, which is built into the nature of attachments, there will, because of the Transonic sacrifice, be other things to take control of; for control is a Transonic thing.

By realizing the Transonic nature of control, one comes to control without controlling. Such is the nature of the rule of God throughout the universe of universes.

As there is none else other than God in all of creation, God must relinquish rule and receive it back reconciled with non-rule. That is, God becomes or is both the ruler and the ruled within the everlasting Kingdom of God.

In the Kingdom that is without beginning or end, the ruler of it is without beginning or end. Thus, the rule exists as a cause and effect relationship to non-rule.

Thus, the Transonic ruler of the universe, by nature of what the ruler must be, rules without ruling. Any other rule is a fleeting thing. Thus, to rule or reign with Christ is to rule in accord with the nature of what rule is in the being of God.

CHAPTER THIRTEEN

The Living Christ

By experiencing the appearing of the living Christ into one's consciousness, one sees the Christ as is, and becomes like unto the Christ of one's being in God.

By seeing the Christ as is, one realizes that it's the Christ of one's being in God that delivers all things unto God. One experiences the Transonic reality of giving all to God, and the Transonic reality of having all returned.

Thus, giving and receiving are realized to be Transonic parts of the same thing in the Consciousness of God. One comes to realize how it is that God is all in all, for one experiences it in consciousness.

That is, the giving and the receiving in the Consciousness of God is ever going on moment by moment. Thus, everything is being delivered unto God and being returned continuously. All things are always surrendered unto God in the Consciousness of God.

Breathing in and breathing out is an example of the giving and receiving interaction in the Consciousness of God. By realizing the Transonic nature of one's being in God, one surrenders all unto God, for it is the God within you surrendering all things unto God.

To live, move, and have being in God consciously is to be aware of what the Consciousness of God is. By receiving the revelation of the Consciousness of God through the living Christ, one becomes aware of what the Consciousness of God is.

That is, one becomes aware of the Consciousness of that which is without beginning or end, the Consciousness of all things. One becomes conscious of the all in all of God within one's being in God.

The all in all of one's being in God is revealed to be that which is both the giver and receiver of all. The all in all of being is not attached to itself, or of anything within the creation of itself.

That is, the all in all of being in God is attached to all things in the universe without being attached to anything. Attachment and detachment are transonically the same thing in the Consciousness of God.

In the all in all of being, it is the nature of being to continuously deliver all unto God, and have it returned purified. In the all in all of being, it is realized that all parts of being are interacting within themselves in perfect Transonic harmony.

Within the interaction of the parts of one's being in God, there is order there, even though it may appear as chaos; for in the Consciousness of God, chaos and order are transonically the same thing. Chaos and order are one hidden in the other, just as destruction and creation are one hidden in the other, which means that the one cancels the other without doing it.

There is neither positive nor negative in the Consciousness of God, for the one serves the purpose of both. Order and chaos, creation and destruction are appearances of the mind of duality, which is not reconciled with the mind of the all in all of being.

To judge by appearances is to deny what things are in the Transonic reality of God. To deliver the things that appear to be unto God through the Christ of one's being in God is to have them returned with the revelation of what they are in the Transonic reality of God.

Anything that is not consciously delivered unto God appears to be separate from God, which denies that God is the all in all of being.

As one learns the nature of the giving and receiving in the Consciousness of God, one learns to surrender all things unto God, for that is the very nature of one's being in God in the first place.

By seeing the Consciousness of the living Christ in another, one becomes like unto the Christ. Therefore, it is realized that there are many, as it were, appearing with the living Christ.

That is, those who become like unto the Christ, by realizing the Christ as the Christ is, join the ranks of the living Christ. Thus, one cannot say the Christ is here or there to the exclusion of: being somewhere else.

The Christ is not something separate form anything, for the Christ dwells in the heart of all things. It is ever the mission of the realized Christ to awaken the Christ within another. It is a matter giving birth to the daystar that is within you.

The living Christ, the daystar of one's being in God has always been with you, as promised. It is the duality of the mind that makes the Christ at the core of being to appear to go away. The Christ, the Lord of being is always a Transonic part and whole of you.

By reconciling the seeming opposites of one's being, the Christ is revealed to be that which links the opposites of being together into a threefold seamless whole.

Thus, the Christ of one's being in God cannot really leave you, for it is there even when it is hidden from consciousness. Even when one is unaware of the Christ within, one has no life apart from the Christ, for the Christ is what allows the opposites to exist in the first place.

That is, opposites exist without existing, for they exist in relation one to the other, and both exist in relation to the third part, the core of being, the neutronic part of one's being in God.

The opposites of being are purified as they are allowed to go through the core of being, for there they are united with their source.

By uniting with the core of being, one learns to interact within one's triune being. One comes to see the flaming fire of the living Christ as it is, which is the purifying agent, the balancing factor of one's being in God.

Thus, the flaming fire of the living Christ is not fire as fire would appear to be, for it is the fire within one's consciousness in God. The fire burns away, purifies all that enters it. The things that need to be burned away or purified are the things built upon the foundation of duality, for they are self-destructive in the first place.

The fire of the Christ of one's being in God purifies the mind of the illusions and attachments to the things of duality. It's a catharsis, an emotional purification, a purging of the mind of duality.

Thus, the cleansing fire of one's being in God is not some outside force, for it is a part of one's being in God.

By realizing that another has gone through the fire of being, one is more prepared to face the fire of one's being in God. Thus, on the one hand, it is a fearful thing, but on the other, it is not a fearful, but the reconciliation of the two.

The fire of being is what one faces unconsciously until one is prepared to face it consciously. To face the fire consciously is to be present at the creation, as it were, for one goes through the destruction and the creation in awareness, and comes out realizing that creation and destruction are Transonic parts of the same thing in the Consciousness of God.

CHAPTER FOURTEEN

Planetary Salvation

With an understanding of the threefold interaction within one's being in God, one realizes the nature of the fall and the rise, for it is realized that the fall and the rise takes place within one's being in God.

The nature of the fall and the rise is such that there is no way to directly explain how either take place, for in Transonic fact, neither can take place, for the fall and the rise are both Transonic parts of one's being in God. The fall and the rise are transonically the same process of expanding the Kingdom of God.

That is, when one is interacting within one's threefold consciousness, the rising and falling is an integrated function of that threefold consciousness. It's just that the rising and falling interact in transonically perfect, Transonic harmony in the balanced threefold consciousness.

Thus, the rising and falling is a part of one's being in God; therefore, it is without beginning or end. Accordingly, one cannot simply say when where, or how the fall takes place.

By following the historical teachings concerning the fall, one is led to the final realization of what the everlasting living Christ is.

By realizing that one is Christ's and Christ is God's, and that God is the all in all of being, one realizes that the fall and rise takes place within the being of God.

The fall and rise is revealed as the creative process in the being of God. It's not that the fall or the rise is good or bad, but that it's there as a part of one's Being in God.

Since the fall and the rise are both a part of one's being in God, there is no reason for not becoming aware of the process of it taking place within ones being in God.

However, we cannot be directly aware of the process, for the process is without beginning or end; and, therefore, transcends awareness without doing it.

That is, one becomes aware of the creative process without becoming aware of it, for awareness and unawareness are transonically the same thing in the Consciousness of God.

The process of the fall and rise is transonically realized when all is delivered unto God, and God is realized to be the all in all of being. That is, as one experiences the rise out of duality by means of the reconciliation of all things unto God through Christ, one sees the connection that unites the opposites together into the one threefold Consciousness.

That is, one realizes that the process is taking place within one's threefold being in God. One finds the way of returning to the garden of God, as it were. One finds the way to be a part of one's being in God.

Thus, by realizing the nature of the rise from the bondage of duality, one can realize what the reversal of that process would be. The reversal of the process would be the gradual falling away from the threefold interaction of one's being in God.

Accordingly, one gradually fell away from the Christ of one's being in God. By falling away from the Christ Consciousness, one is rejecting the capstone of the temple of God, which is one's body.

By rejecting, although unconsciously, the Christ of one's being in God, one unconsciously fell into the conflict of opposites.

By rejecting the unifying factor of one's being, one ejects oneself from the Consciousness of God into the realm of duality, into the conflict of what appears as good and evil.

In the realm of duality, the fall and the rise appear to be in conflict, and one comes under the illusion of opposites. The falling and rising becomes the cycle of birth and death in the realm of duality.

As one fell from a part of one's being in God, the only way back is through the rejected part of being, the living Christ of one's being in God.

Christ is the stone that was disallowed, and is made the head of the corner. By rejecting the Christ of one's being in God, one suffers the consequences of that until one realizes that one has done that rejecting.

By falling from the Christ of one's being in God, one fell from God. Thus, the only way back is to reverse the process. When it is said that the Christ is the way, the truth, and the life, it is realized that the living Christ represents what you are in the fullness of God.

Christ is the door, not as something outside you, but the door within your being in God. There is no other way back to God because of the cause and effect relationship within the fall and rise. The fall and the rise cannot be separated, for they are Transonic parts of the same thing.

The door into duality and the door out of it is the same door, the Christ of one's being in God. Thus, one must return through the same door one came through in first place.

By realizing the nature of the return to God, one realizes how the planet is to be returned to God for purification. By delivering all unto God through Christ by means of the reconciliation of the opposites of one's being in God, the planetary Consciousness is affected.

Turning the planet back to God is not an optional thing, for the planet is God's, shared by all upon it. Turning the planet back to God is not doing God a favor as though God were something separate from you.

It is the mind of God within you that reveals the need to return the planet back to God for purification, for you are just as much a part of the planet as God is.

Just as the fall into duality is a process that transcends time, the process of returning the earth back to God is a process that transcends time.

The past warnings concerning the course of a fallen planet tends to go unheeded because of the lack of understanding what is happening. It's not easy to reveal how that duality is ever on a self-destructive course.

The mind of duality has, as it were, the world set in its heart. It knows not how it got into its situation, or how to get out of it. The Christ of one's being in God is the deliverer out of such a situation.

By seeing the Christ deliverer in another, one awakens to the deliverer within one's being in God.

As each awakened one returns all things unto God through Christ, the planet is being returned to God through Christ. It is the reconciliation of all things unto God through Christ that is the means of rising the planetary Consciousness, and bringing it in line with those that are already doing so.

The earth can be transformed back to its balanced harmony by reversing the process of what brought it to its unbalanced condition. It's the same process in reverse. The reversal of the process is inevitable one way or the other, for a destructive course of nature destroys itself if not turned around in time to avoid it, which is something that a little child could very well tell you.

As the individuals of a planet consciously or unconsciously move within the Consciousness of the reconciliation of all things unto God through the Christ of one's being in God, the planetary return becomes an experience shared by all.

Everybody is a participant in the return of the planet to God, for we are all co-workers in the Kingdom of God whether we know it or not. We must work either consciously or unconsciously within it, for the Kingdom includes both the conscious and the unconscious nature of things. That is, the conscious and the unconscious are transonically the same thing in the Consciousness of God.

CHAPTER FIFTEEN

Total Awareness

By realizing and becoming the Transonic sacrifice, and delivering all things unto God, the all in all of God is realized, and the mystery of God is thereby finished.

That is, the mystery of God is finished, in that it is revealed that God was not a mystery in the first place. The mystery and the revelation of God are transonically the same thing.

The simplicity and the mystery concerning God has been an illusion of the dual mind. That is, the dual mind sees God as either simple or complex.

By realizing that the little child is as apt to understand the mystery of God as the most intellectual is, one is in the position to become aware of what the mystery of God is.

The Consciousness of God is as simple as anything can get, for it is the Consciousness of all things from the lowest to the highest.

It is just that the Consciousness of God is not what it appears to be, and that one must sacrifice the appearance of things in order to become aware of what God is.

To think that God is far away or beyond one's understanding is to be under an illusion as to what God is, for you have no understanding apart from God's understanding.

That is, one is using the mind of God even when one is doing so unconsciously. That is how one comes to experience the mind of God consciously. What one does unconsciously in God, one comes to do it consciously later.

Therefore, when the reversal from doing things in God unconsciously takes place, it is just the change from unconsciousness to consciousness in the Being of God.

By reconciling the conscious and the unconscious awareness, the mystery of God disappears. One, while trapped in duality, tends to forgets that one is, indeed, created in the image or in accord with the nature of God.

God and everything in the creation of God is created in God; that is, all things are created in accord with the pattern of the one thing.

There is nothing that can get out of the creation of God, for one cannot get out of it by getting out of it. Such is the seeming contradiction in the nature of all things. That is, the all in all of being takes in the inside and the outside of all things, for the inside and the outside are transonically the same thing in the Consciousness of God.

By reconciling the opposites of one's being unto God through the Christ of Being, one experiences the Consciousness of God to be neither simple nor complex.

It is the reconciliation of the simple and the complex that makes the Consciousness of God available to all.

To present God as simple is to deny the complex nature of God; and to present God as complex is to deny the simple nature of God.

Thus, it is not enough to say that God is simple or relative without relating that to the complex or absolute nature of God, and vice versa.

The relative and the absolute nature of God are Transonic parts of the same thing, just as the simple and the complex are transonically the same thing.

Thus, one must be led from the simple to the complex, for God is not found in the simple. Then one must be led from the complex to the simple, for God is not found in the complex. That, of course, is the cycle of birth and death of the simple and the complex.

It is when one comes to realize that one has been caught up in the cycle, and looks for the deliverer out it, that one is led to reconcile the opposites of one's being in God, which is the way of finishing the mystery of God within one's being in God.

By reconciling all things unto God, one comes to realize that the Consciousness of God does not change, and that one has been dwelling in that Consciousness all along in unawareness.

Although the Consciousness of God is available to all, in that it is the Consciousness of all, none are forced into the conscious awareness of it.

However, by avoiding entering the promised land of being, the Consciousness of God, through fear of what it might be is still to bring what is feared upon one unconsciously, for what one cannot face consciously, one must do so unconsciously; for that is the manner of training in the Consciousness of God.

One can handle the total awareness of God because the total awareness of God is not what it might appear to be. Total awareness and total unawareness are transonically the same thing in the Consciousness of God.

Thus, the seemingly unbearable burden of total awareness is shared by the unawareness within the awareness. In the Consciousness of God, one has total awareness without having total awareness, for there is neither awareness nor unawareness in the Consciousness of God, for the one cancels the other.

Thus, the awareness and the unawareness are parts of one's threefold, seamless Consciousness in God, which is a multiple extension of itself to Transonic infinity.

Just as one has a body within a body to Transonic infinity, yet uses one body for a given purpose, one has awareness within awareness to Transonic infinity. One uses the awareness focused within the given body.

Thus, it's not a matter of trying to become aware of all things in the universe as though one must have awareness scattered all over the universe. It only appears that total awareness should expand all at once. It doesn't expand all at once, for it is not what it appears to be.

To claim total awareness is to deny the unawareness hidden in it. However, the nature of total awareness is such that one can have it, but in accord with the nature of what it is in the Consciousness of God, not what it appears to be.

That is, by putting awareness through the Transonic sacrifice of the Christ of one's being in God, one receives it back reconciled with unawareness. One can handle that total awareness of God, for both the mystery of it, and the burden of it is lifted and borne, as it were, by the living Christ of one's being in God.

Accordingly, each individual in the being of God is led to bear the total burden of creation by doing it transonically; that is, by doing it without doing it.

However, as each bears the burden individually, it is still in the nature of things to find that all other individuals share the same burden individually. Thus, one bears the burden alone, yet shares it with the whole of creation.

CHAPTER SIXTEEN

Total Awareness II

The individual and the universal being are seen to be the same being. By nature of being an individual in the being of God, one has transcended the individuality of oneself without doing it.

Just as God is transonically linked to every other individual in the universe, every other individual is transonically linked to every other individual in the universe. Thus, the individuality of each is as the individuality of God, and the individuality of God transcends itself without doing it.

Thus, one is not called upon to bear what another is not called upon to bear in the Consciousness of God. However, the Consciousness of God will not seem bearable until one reconciles the seeming opposites of one's being in God.

The infinity of God cannot be realized until the infinite is reconciled with the finite. One can no more find God in the infinite than one can find God in the finite, for God is the Transonic reconciliation of the infinite and the finite, transcending both without transcending either.

Thus, the infinite is not what it might appear to be, and the finite is not what it might appear to be, for they are transonically the same thing in the Transonic Consciousness of God.

The infinite and the finite are parts of one's being in God, which are transonically sacrificed in the being of God.

Accordingly, one moves the finite as one moves toward infinity. Thus, one is not moving toward infinity, for one is moving infinity as one moves in it. One cannot move toward or away from something that is without beginning or end.

Accordingly, one moves, without moving, the entire universe of universes as one moves in the being of God. Thus, the infinity of God is within the range of the little child's understanding.

In like manner, the omnipresence of God is transonically understandable, for the everywhereness of God is a Transonic part of the nowhereness of God.

The reconciliation of being everywhere and nowhere is as the reconciliation of being and nonbeing. Thus, to be transonically everywhere is to be at one point that can transfer to another point to Transonic infinity.

By sacrificing being everywhere, one appears at one point, and by sacrificing the one point, one can transfer from point to point to anywhere in the universe, for the one point is a multiple threefold extension of itself to Transonic infinity.

One could say that one individual moves from point to point, and in that sense be potentially everywhere, yet in relation to one's Transonic link to universal being, one is represented everywhere as well.

One can also say that one is neither at one point, nor everywhere, in that one ever transcends both positions without doing it, for it is the interaction of being transcendent, yet immanent within all things.

In that God is without beginning or end, yet appears to be the end and beginning of all things, one comes to realize that God only appears to be without beginning or end, for God cannot be simply what one might say God is.

Thus, God is without beginning or end without being so. God is without beginning or end, in that the end and the beginning are transonically the same thing.

Thus, there are ends and beginnings in God as to the appearance of things. That is, everything that lives and dies in God appears to begin and end, but neither the beginning nor the end ever take place, in that the beginning and the end are the same thing in the Consciousness of God.

That is, just as the infinite and the finite move together, yet separately, the beginning and end move together, yet separately; for they can neither come together nor be separated.

Things end and begin without ending or beginning, for the one exists only in relation to the other. Thus, the end and beginning of things are as the one thing that is a threefold multiple of itself to Transonic infinity.

Thus, things appear to begin and end as through they were separate things until the beginning and end of things are reconciled through the Christ of one's being in God. Then things are seen to end without ending, and to begin without beginning, for that was what they were doing in the first place.

Thus, the beginninglessness and the endlessness of one's being in God is understandable by means of the reconciliation, by seeing the two parts of being as parts of the same thing. One is thus relieved of the burden of trying to understand something that is not really there in the first place, as it appears to be.

One understands things in the being of God by not understanding them. That is, there is nothing in the being of God that is supposed to be understood, in that what is not understood is a Transonic part of what is.

Thus, by losing one's understanding in God, one receives it back reconciled with non-understanding. To understand all that God is, one must understand all that God is not, and then reconcile that in order to realize God in Transonic reality.

God is all that is, and all that is not, without being either, for what God is and what God is not are transonically the same thing. To realize that what is and what is not are the same thing, one must realize the Transonic sacrifice in the nature of one's being in God. What is and what is not are cause and effect to one another; therefore, neither are what they appear to be.

Thus, it is God that calls things from out of seeming nothing to be what they appear to be. It is God that can call the things that appear to be back into seeming nothingness.

Although that might appear a complicated thing, it is not, in that God has been doing that within you, and within all things from before the foundation of the world.

That is, one has been going through the process of coming to be out of seeming nothing, but in unawareness. Becoming aware of it doesn't change the nature of it. One understands the Consciousness of God by understanding one's consciousness in God, for they are the same thing. The Creator and the created are cause and effect to one another.

Thus, it's not that God cannot be described, or understood. It's a matter of understanding God in accord with the nature of God, which is to understand and to describe without understanding, or describing.

What appears as knowledge is knowledge in part. One receives the knowledge of God when knowledge in part is done away in Transonic knowledge. By transonically transcending what appears as knowledge, one finds the knowledge of God bearable, for it doesn't carry the burden of what appears as knowledge does.

In the Consciousness of God, the knowledge of one thing contains the knowledge of all things. Thus, the knowledge of God can be condensed to a point, or into one word that is a threefold expansion of itself to Transonic infinity.

One cannot escape the responsibility of one's being in God by denying that God exists, for the denial of God is but a part of God that the denier doesn't know is there. There is no existence of anything apart from God.

It is the Consciousness of God within the denier of God that denies God as a means of experiencing that side of the nature of God, which only points to the Transonic fact that God is the Transonic denier of God, in that God denies without denying, for God is immanent, yet transcendent of itself. God doesn't claim to be God, nor does God claim not to be God, for claiming something in the Consciousness of God is a denial of it.

CHAPTER SEVENTEEN

The All-Comprehensive Goal

By having faith in the one goal that includes all goals, one is led to the awareness of that goal within one's consciousness in God. To find the one thing that contains all things is to find the one goal that includes all goals.

To find the one thing that includes all things is to transcend the need to search for anything, for the searcher and what is searched for become one in the Consciousness of God.

By having faith that the Kingdom of God includes all things, one is led to the Transonic verification of that in one's consciousness in God, for the Kingdom represents the one thing that includes all things. However, the nature of the Kingdom is such that it is not easy to find, for it is not what it might appear to be.

That is, the Kingdom is that, having found, one gives all for. As the Kingdom represents all, what ones gives for it represents all.

Accordingly, the price of the Kingdom is the Transonic sacrifice of one's being in God, for the Transonic sacrifice represents the redemption of all things from before the foundation of the world.

Therefore, the price of the Kingdom includes the giving up what the kingdom might appear to be. One must give up thinking that the Kingdom has a beginning or end, for it is as God, without beginning or end.

Thus, finding the Kingdom is finding God, for both represent the all in all of being. The Christ, the Kingdom, the Transonic sacrifice, and God all represent the one thing that is without beginning or end.

By realizing that the one thing in God represents all things, one realizes that all things in the universe are related to the one goal of finding the Kingdom that is from before the foundation of the world.

Accordingly, all things are, as it were, added to the finding of the one thing, for all things were already added to it, but one wasn't aware of it before finding it.

Finding the Kingdom, and overcoming death both represent the final goal, for both require the giving of all. Just as one finds life by losing it, one finds the Kingdom by losing it; for the nature of the Kingdom and of life is such that neither are lost in the first place, but only appeared to be.

That is, neither the Kingdom nor life are lost because both are from before the foundation of the world; and, therefore, are without beginning or end.

Accordingly, to lose the Kingdom is to find it, and to find it is to lose it, for the losing and the finding are transonically the same thing.

Thus, to lose life is to find it, and to find it is lose it, for losing is finding and finding is losing. Just as losing and finding are the same thing, life and death are the same thing. One opposite is the other in reverse.

Accordingly, neither the Kingdom nor life nor anything in the universe can be either lost or found, for what is lost is forever linked to what is found, and what is found is forever linked to what is lost, for the one is the Transonic cause and the effect of the other.

Thus, one cannot find the one thing that includes all things by searching in the realm of duality, for things appear to be separated from one another in the realm of duality.

The realm of duality is the realm of sinners that need, as it were, a physician that transcends the cause and effect relationship of the dual mind. The giving of all in purchasing the Kingdom includes the entire realm of duality, the entire realm of creation.

That is, the Kingdom takes in more that the realm of creation. The Kingdom is beyond the conflict of opposites in the realm of duality.

That is, the Kingdom takes one out of the cycle of birth and death of the realm of duality. The mind of Christ sees from beyond the context of the conflict of opposites.

Thus, the mind of duality is the natural mind that cannot discern the things of the Spirit of God, for it knows not what the Spirit of God is.

There is none good in the realm of duality, for the good and evil there are cause and effect to one another. Thus, good and evil both come under the giving of all things in purchasing the Kingdom.

The Christ is beyond the good and evil of duality, for the Christ is the Transonic reconciliation of good and evil; that is, the Christ burns away, as it were, all within duality that cannot enter the Consciousness of God.

Thus, the one goal is related to all things in the realm of duality, for the one goal is the way out of duality. Everything in the universe is related to the one goal, for it includes all things from before the foundation of the world.

As one finds the Kingdom by losing it, and finds life by losing it, one is functioning in the mind of God that transcends itself without doing it.

That is, God finds things by losing them, and loses them by finding them, for that is the nature of the mind God in you, and within all things.

Thus, we come to realize that finding the Christ is finding a part of the overall goal. That is, the goal of the appearing of the Christ within one's consciousness, becoming like unto the Christ, is a goal within the goal of goals.

That is, one must become fully aware of what it is that one has become by becoming like unto the Christ, for there are many versions as to what the Christ might be.

Thus, becoming like unto the Christ is as a new beginning in relation to the overall goal in the Consciousness of God. Therefore, as one becomes the living Christ, the living Christ becomes the Reconciler of all things unto God.

Thus, the new beginning becomes the age of the reconciliation, the promised millennial reign of Christ when the wolf and lamb of being dwell in harmony, where the Word of the Lord flows like a river unto all.

The age of the reconciliation is the age of delivering the Kingdom unto God. Thus, in the reconciliation, we each individually and all collectively participate in the process of delivering the Kingdom unto God.

One can see that delivering the Kingdom is a goal within a goal, for one can see beyond to when all is delivered unto God, and God is realized to be the all in all in the being of all in the Consciousness of God.

As the Christ within one delivers all unto God, the Christ receives it back, and thereby realizes that giving and receiving the Kingdom are transonically the same thing in the Consciousness of God.

The Christ within one realizes the Consciousness of God by acting in accord with the nature of it; that is, one learns by experiencing it.

It is when the Christ realizes the nature of the Consciousness of God to be both the giver and the receiver, that the Christ becomes subject to what one can have no doubt, or lack of confidence in; for it is God being subject to God, for God is realized to be the all in all of being; for that is, and was the nature of God, and of all things in the first place.

Thus, the goal of becoming aware of the all in all of being is the one goal that includes all things from before and after itself, for it is without beginning or end.

Therefore, the goal that allows no other is the goal of the eternal day of God that is from everlasting to everlasting. In the all in all of being in God, all things are transonically sacrificed, for God gives all to the creation as the creation can receive it.

By means of the process of becoming aware of God, one becomes aware that God is the Transonic sacrifice within all things. As God is the Transonic sacrifice, all things of creation are created as self-sacrificing things.

What becomes aware of God is God becoming aware of God in God's Consciousness, for there is none else. One loses God in order to realize what God is in Transonic reality. God is lost and found within God, for there is nowhere else for God to be found or lost.

Thus, one loses God by finding God, and finds God by losing God, for God can be neither lost nor found, for God is both without being either.

One loses and finds God within oneself in God, for it is God finding and losing God within you. God is the giver of givers, and the receiver of receivers. The nature of God is such that God is hidden in creation, and creation is hidden in God. Thus, the Creator finds itself in the creature, and the creatures finds itself in God, for the one is hidden in the other.

The Creator and the created are transonically the same thing in the Consciousness of God. God is neither creator nor created, in that God is the Transonic reconciliation of the Creator and the created.

God sacrifices the role of Creator and becomes the created, and sacrifices the role of the created and becomes the Creator.

Thus, both the Creator and the created are transonically transcended in the Consciousness of God, for God, being without beginning or end, transcends what God might appear to be.

Thus, one cannot find any goal beyond the all in all of being in God, for there is nothing to lose or find there, for all was lost and found in getting here, in that there and here are transonically the same thing in the Consciousness of God, which is the goal of all things, for it is the Transonic goal of God.

The End

WORLD WITHOUT END

*THE MANY MANSIONS
OF BEING
WITHIN YOU*

CHAPTER ONE

One World In Many

To reconcile the seeming contradiction in the biblical expression that speaks of the *world without end* is to reconcile the seeming contradiction in the nature of all things, for the nature of one thing is as the nature of all things in the Transonic Consciousness of God, which is transcendent of all things, including Itself, without being transcendent of anything in the universe of universes.

One cannot realize how the world is without end until one also realizes that it is also without beginning; for the end and the beginning are two parts of the same thing, which is to say the one exists in relation to the other. Accordingly, neither the beginning nor the end of anything has existence as it would appear.

One cannot expect another to explain how it is that the world is without beginning or end, for it is not something that one is supposed to understand apart from one's own consciousness, for one's consciousness is that which is without beginning or end.

That is, the world that is without beginning or end is a projection of the consciousness that is without beginning or end, which is to say all things conform to the pattern of the one Consciousness of God, which is without beginning or end.

Accordingly, the individual atoms that make up the universal body of God all conform to the pattern of being without beginning or end, for atoms have neither beginning nor end, for that is the nature of atoms in the creation of God in the first place.

The world is without beginning or end, yet it appears to have both because the one world is one world in many worlds, and many worlds in one world.

That is, the one world is a multiple of itself to Transonic infinity. Accordingly, no world can be considered the beginning or end, for it forever dwells in the context of that which is without beginning or end.

The one world is the world of the many mansions, as it were, which are the many worlds within the one world.

Although one cannot rely on the word of another concerning the many mansions, one can, when prepared to do so, experience first hand the many mansions, for the many mansions are a part of one's being in the Consciousness of God.

Innerworld travel is not a complicated thing as it would appear, for it, being a part of one's being, one experiences it unconsciously long before one is prepared to do it consciously.

The ideal way of gaining the conscious awareness of innerworld travel is to find one that has experienced consciously innerworld travel, and receive whatever instructions and assistance that one needs to experience innerworld travel.

It is best receive preparation and assistance, or to be aware that it is there, for one is becoming aware and facing one's so-called good and bad side in the Being of God.

Thus, the time of preparation is one of purifying one's consciousness, of maintaining a balance in order to deal with what one might find in the inner worlds.

The process of soul travel is a means of relating to the nonexistence of death. It confirms the Truth that to lose life is to save it. Through soul travel, one gets the realization that life and death are transonically the same thing, interchangeable one through the other.

One also experiences first hand the reality hidden in illusion, and the illusion hidden in reality. That is, when one moves out of the so-called real world to an inner world, the inner world appears to be the real world; moreover, when one moves from an inner world to a higher inner world, the higher inner world is the one that appears real.

Therefore, as there are worlds within worlds without end, one can go from one world to another; and have each world appear to be the real world until it dawns on one that no world can be considered the real world to the exclusion of any other world.

One comes to realize that the one world is transonically linked to an infinite number of worlds without beginning or end. The death of one world is the birth of another, for the other is but a part of the one world. Thus the world only appears to die, for the so-called death is a part of the life of it.

That is, when one leaves the body in the sleep state, the outer world seems to disappear, and an inner world appears as an outer world. Yet when one returns to the body, the outer world is still there. Accordingly, the worlds of the one world coexist without interfering with one another.

Thus, one can appear to die to one body, and appear to move within an inner world within another body, yet return to the body.

As there is a world within one to Transonic infinity, there is a body within one to Transonic infinity, whether it form or formless be. That is, there is a formless and a form body, which are two parts of the same thing.

As you transcend yourself and find yourself in God, you attune to the vibrations of that world. Thus, the one body of God is a body that is a threefold, Transonic multiple of itself to Transonic infinity.

The body of God, which is the body of all things, is set within the context of that which is without beginning or end. Thus, those who go into the inner planes of God to find the absolute or the end find neither, for God has neither beginning nor end; therefore, nothing in the universe of God has a beginning or end, for all things must conform to the pattern within the Consciousness of God.

Such is the reason there is perfect order in the realms of God, even though there may appear to be chaos; for nothing can deviate from the pattern of the Consciousness of God, for the so-called deviation is but a part of the perfection of the pattern in the Consciousness of God. The perfection of God is Transonic, and not what it appears to be.

Although it would appear impossible to develop a consciousness that is without beginning or end, one finds that it is impossible to develop one that has a beginning or end, for one cannot find the beginning or the end of anything.

Therefore, one is ever doing the impossible, for one is living, moving, and having being in the Consciousness that is without beginning or end; for to do otherwise would be to predate God, which is also seemingly impossible in that God predates Itself.

Thus, the Consciousness that one is using transcends both the beginning and the end within itself, without doing it, in that it is both the beginning and the end of itself without being either.

Accordingly, as one is created in the Consciousness of God, one cannot find the beginning or end anywhere outside oneself, for the end and the beginning are but parts of oneself that only appear to be.

In the Consciousness of God, all things are a threefold unity, the parts of which are immanent, yet transcendent in the other, with the threefold unity or the whole being a multiple of Itself to Transonic infinity. However, that information may be conscious or unconscious. It is a matter of each cell in the body of God becoming aware of what it is in the Consciousness of God.

Thus, the conscious and the unconscious in the Consciousness of God are without beginning or end, for they are parts of the same thing in the Being of God.

As one transcends oneself and finds oneself in God, it is God doing that in you. Thus, God in you realizes the beginningless and the endless nature of Itself, and of all things within Itself. Thus, as you are immanent, yet transcendent in God, God is immanent, yet transcendent in you. As you see yourself in God, God sees Itself in you.

CHAPTER TWO

Worlds Of Duality

Until one realizes the purpose of the worlds of duality, one feels little need to find the way that leads one beyond them.

The worlds of duality are the worlds where life and death move in cycles without one realizing that such is so. Thus, one becomes trapped in the realm of duality without knowing one is trapped. Any attempt to deliver one from the bondage of duality is generally opposed by the ones trapped there.

Thus, the one with the message of deliverance is never accepted by the masses, for none know what the deliverance is, for none know the nature of their bondage.

However, that is as it should be, in that the worlds of duality are as a training school that is meant to prepare one for the worlds beyond.

That is, one needs to overcome the duality within one's nature in God before going beyond the worlds of duality. It is in the physical aspect of the realm of duality that one has the opportunity of overcoming death, which is overcoming duality within one's nature.

It is in overcoming the duality of one's being that one becomes aware of the threefold nature of one's being in God.

As one reconciles the duality of one's being, one is transforming the nature of oneself as well as the world around one. Thus, as the many within the one of a planetary body reconcile the opposites within the world itself is transformed and becomes a part of the glorious liberty of the children of God.

Until the masses are made to realize their part in the creation of the world around them, and stop rejecting the message of deliverance, the liberty of the children of God is delayed, without anyone knowing how that is.

However, inasmuch as the deliverance is an individual as well as a universal thing, and takes place in the physical body, there are many living now who have already received the glorious liberation.

Therefore, it is a matter of those liberated ones coming out of hiding, so to speak, and lending support to the messenger of the liberation. There is a time for everything under the sun, a time for the rejected ones to reveal themselves, and a time for the ones that have rejected them to acknowledge that they have done so.

It is not that this would be anything new, for it goes on at one measure or level or another. It is a matter of what is right for the purpose of the time.

Thus, the possibility of this happening should not be a surprise, for the world has been prepared for such an event. It fact, it would seem that the world, as a whole, would be disappointed if such an event didn't happen within their lifetime.

It is not that anything can disrupt what must be. It is a matter of what must be coming to be. That is, what is to happen is what is programmed in accord with the cause and effect relationship within the world as a whole.

It is the action or reaction that the world takes in relation to the messenger of Truth that brings the judgment upon the world.

That is, what is done unto the Lord reflects back to one, whether good or bad. Thus, to see the Lord as *is* is to become like unto the Lord, and to enjoy all that the Lord is. To see the Lord as something the Lord is not is to become that, not knowing what the Lord is.

Thus, to reject the messenger of the message that transcends duality is to remain in the realm of duality until one is prepared to see the Lord as is, and to be led out of the bondage of duality.

As the realm of duality is the realm of birth and death, to reject the Truth of being is to choose to remain in the realm of duality, which is choosing the second death, as it were.

As the realm of duality is self-destructive by the nature of itself, it is a mark of wisdom to seek a way of resolving the conflict and return to the realm of the threefold consciousness.

However, after one has resolved the conflict, it becomes easier to remain in the realm of duality in order to help any seeking help in overcoming the conflict of opposites.

Accordingly, many have returned from the higher worlds to offer assistance to those trapped in duality, for the lower worlds are a part of the higher in the first place.

Thus, there is always one to assist one, as one is ready for that assistance of overcoming the worlds of duality, for one is transonically linked to that assistance; thus, assistance must come when one is ready for it.

Once one overcomes the opposites within one's being in the world of duality, one is said to be in the world, yet not of it. It is a matter of maintaining the balance of opposites once the balance is realized.

By maintaining the balance of opposites, one is thereby consciously absorbing that balance within one's present consciousness, which one moves with one as a part of one's omnipresent Consciousness.

Thus, there is no point in trying to get beyond one's consciousness, for it cannot get beyond itself, for it is already beyond itself no matter where it is.

By realizing that one's present consciousness is linked to one's omnipresent Consciousness, one is conscious of one's present consciousness while traveling in the inner worlds.

By moving consciously out of the waking state, and moving through the inner worlds, one is registering an identity on the various planes of being.

Thus, one attains to an identity within the Consciousness of God, which is an identity that's in accord with the nature of God; and not what it would appear to be, for one's identity in God transcends itself without doing it.

That is, to identify with God as God is in Transonic reality is to identify with that which is without beginning or end; therefore, such identity cannot be what it might appear to be, for one comes to be without being in the Being of God.

Every being is the part and the whole of the Being of God, yet being is transonically transcended in the Being of God.

Thus, to identify with God is to identify with all things without identifying with anything. One therefore becomes attached to all things without becoming attached to anything, for that is the nature of the Consciousness that is without beginning or end.

The Consciousness that is without beginning or end cannot be destroyed; therefore, it is the everlasting Consciousness of the everlasting Kingdom of God, which is without beginning or end.

The Consciousness that is without beginning or end is neither attached to or detached from anything in the universe. Thus, by moving within that awareness of itself, Consciousness cannot become bound to anything, and is therefore free in that context.

Such freedom is realized to be Transonic, for both so-called freedom and bondage are transcended in the Transonic freedom of God. Such freedom is beyond understanding, for it is supposed to be.

Thus, the freedom in God cannot even be called freedom. Accordingly, the power of God is not what it might appear to be; for the power that is all power must transcend all power, which is done in the Consciousness of God.

Nothing can go against the power of God, for there is nothing there that one can find to go against. It has already overcome all power by becoming what It is.

Thus, the transonically infinite freedom and power of God is linked to the transonically infinite wisdom of God, all as a part of one function.

CHAPTER THREE

Lower Worlds

By traveling through the inner worlds and returning to the body, one comes to realize that the many worlds are transonically linked together.

One comes to realize that for every lower world there is a higher, and vice versa, for the one is a Transonic part of the other.

The lower worlds and the higher worlds are all a part of the same world. As one goes to the so-called higher world, the higher world is realized to be a lower world of yet a higher world.

Accordingly, one can never find the end of the outer world, nor can one find the end to the inner world, for there is no end to find; for there is not supposed to be in a world without end.

As there are outer worlds of duality, there are inner worlds of duality. By reconciling the outer, one is also reconciling the inner.

As one realizes the need as well as the possibility of reconciling all things through Christ unto God, one realizes that all things, indeed, come under the reconciliation.

Accordingly, by reconciling what appears as the lower worlds, one learns that the higher and the lower are parts of the same thing.

Thus, one realizes the possibility of reconciling what appears as the positive spiritual world with what appears as the negative matter world. Thereby one comes to realize that spirit and matter are transonically the same thing.

Thus, by reconciling all things through Christ unto God, God is realized not to be there in the spiritual worlds to the exclusion of being here in the matter worlds, and vice versa.

Therefore, by reconciling all worlds unto the one world without end, one comes to realize how it is that the body of man and woman is, indeed, the body of God.

It is found that it is from within the body of man and woman that God has access to all the worlds within the one world without end.

Accordingly, it is from within the body of all things that God acquires total knowledge of Itself, for it is from within the body of all things that the knowledge of all as well as the knowledge of nothing is learned.

Accordingly, total knowledge of all things in God is not what that knowledge might appear to be to the mind of duality. That is, the total knowledge of all must, by the nature of being total, include the total knowledge of nothing. Thus, to know all, one must be prepared to know nothing.

Knowledge must, as it were, cease before it is realized to be what it is in the Consciousness that is without end or beginning.

It is the beginningless and the endless nature of the Consciousness of God that allows It to be everywhere and nowhere at the same time without being in either places. If that sounds complicated or mysterious, it is just as much due to the simplicity of it as to the mystery of it.

There are no simple or complicated ways to express the inexpressible. The inexpressible is expressed in a threefold way. Thus, there must be an interaction of a threefold expression in order to express the threefold nature of being that has neither beginning nor end.

Accordingly, one needs to reconcile the letter with spirit of the word unto the threefold Word that transcends Itself to Transonic infinity.

By realizing the threefold nature of the Word of God, one realizes that the Word of God is omnipresent throughout the universe of universes; for the threefold Word is a multiple of Itself to Transonic infinity.

Accordingly, all things are transonically linked to the Voice, the Sound, the Word of God whether it is realized or not. It is a matter of becoming conscious of being linked to the everlasting Word of God, and moving in the consciousness of It.

Accordingly, the one who has become conscious of the Word is in position to help another make connection to the Word that is a part of one's being in God.

However, since the Word is a part of one's being, another helps one to help oneself. It is a matter of being prepared to recognize the Word.

It is a matter of becoming aware that one is that Word, for It represents the All in all of Being. It is that Word that is said to become flesh, for It is realized to be within the body of the one expressing it.

The Word, being omnipresent, is with one on all planes of being. The Word is silent, yet audible, unwritten, yet written.

However, by reconciling the silent aspect of It with the audible, it is realized that the sound and the silence are parts of the same thing.

Thus, the Word appears as silence or sound, but is neither in that the one is hidden in the other. Thus, the silence and the sound are one hidden in the other without beginning or end.

There is nowhere for the silence and sound of the Word to come together or apart. By reconciling the sound and silence of the Word, and realizing their Transonic oneness, one realizes the threefold nature of the Word that ends and begins within Itself without ending or beginning.

Once one becomes aware that the Word represents all things in the Consciousness of God, one can condense knowledge into that one Word, which is God.

Thus, the so-called expansion and condensation of the universe is condensed into the one Word, for the expansion is hidden in the condensation, and vice versa. One point becomes equivalent to all points, and all points become equivalent to the one point.

Thus, total knowledge is contained at one point, for all things extend from the one point. Thus, the expansion and the condensation are parts of the same thing, not one thing separate from the other.

To be everywhere and at one point is to be just where you are, for all places are transonically linked together as parts of one place. Thus, there is no such thing as being everywhere or at one point.

That is, everywhere is transonically linked to nowhere. The one exists in relation to the other. One point is transonically linked to all points. The one exists in relation to all, and vice versa.

As one thing is as the nature of all things, which is so because of the pattern in the creation of all things, to realize the nature of one thing is to realize the nature of all things.

Thus, what would be considered a burden, such as holding in consciousness the total knowledge of all things, turns out to be no burden at all, for the burden is borne away in the Consciousness that transcends itself.

The knowledge that is a burden to hold is the knowledge that passes away anyway. The everlasting, Transonic knowledge is not a burden, for it is a knowledge that knows without knowing, and thereby knows all by knowing nothing to be a part of it.

Thus, there is an area within one's being, the Christ Consciousness, that one can unload, as it were, one's burdens, for they are borne away there into nothingness.

Accordingly, the Christ that bears your burdens away is the Christ that is a part of your consciousness in God. This is realized when one sees the Christ as the Christ is, for by seeing the Christ in another, one sees the Christ to be the Self of one's being.

Until one can see the Christ as is in another, the Christ remains hidden in oneself.

The Word of the Christ of God penetrates to the core of one's being in God, and reveals one to oneself. Thus, to hear the Word of God within one's being is to be linked to that Word, which is the way that leads one to the realization of what one is in God.

CHAPTER FOUR

Solar Worlds

By reconciling the seeming opposites of the worlds of duality, one earns the right to enter the worlds transcending duality.

Although there are many descriptions as to what a solar world might be, it's not easy to grasp the meaning of any term that might be used in describing the nature of a solar world.

It is not that there can be anything complicated about what a solar world might be, for whatever the mystery of it might be, there is the simplicity hidden in it.

Accordingly, one may be hindered by the simplicity of it as well as the mystery of it. History has been a lesson in unfolding the solar Consciousness, which is the solar Consciousness within one's being in God.

If one sees the soul as being at the center of the opposites of one's being, soul is seen as the solar Consciousness. Thus, the soul plane of one's being is beyond duality, in that it is the reconciliation of the opposites of duality.

If you see the soul as being at the core of the positive and negative parts of being, then the soul is realized to be the neutron of being.

Thus, the solar, the soul, and the neutronic Consciousness all refer the same thing. Moreover, the Sun of Righteousness refers to the same thing.

Accordingly, the Daystar born within the heart of man refers to the same thing. It is the Consciousness of the flaming fire of the Lord, as it were.

Thus, all the terms referring to the solar Consciousness are but partial descriptions of what It is, which is the Word of God.

The solar Consciousness contains both the silent and the audible Word, for the silent and the audible Word flow through the core of being, the solar Consciousness.

There is a continual flowing in and out through the core of being. It is as two waves passing through one another, which maintains the threefold balance.

The solar Consciousness is also refereed to as the strait gate, the narrow, and the middle way. It is also what the living Christ Consciousness is.

It is through the core of being, the neutronic Christ Consciousness, that the Word of God flows through Itself to all things in the universes.

As the Christ Self at the core of one's being in God is a threefold thing that is a multiple of Itself to Transonic infinity, the Word of God within you is a threefold multiple of Itself to Transonic infinity.

Therefore, the Word flows through that center of one's being, no matter where one might be in the universe, for the center of being is a threefold multiple of itself to Transonic infinity.

Accordingly, the Word of God is omnipresent throughout the universe of universes, for It flows through the center of Itself, which is transonically everywhere; for the center transcends itself without doing it.

Accordingly, just as one cannot find a beginning or end to anything, one cannot find the center of anything, for there is nowhere the center is not.

Thus, as one is linked transonically to the everlasting Word of God, one moves the entire center of all things as one moves. However, such motion is within the omnipresence of being; therefore, one moves the center without moving it.

What appears as motion is but the moving from center to center in the one center that is without beginning or end.

One moves within the omnipresence of one's being in God, the all in all, which is to move without moving. Omnipresence is not what it appears to be, and that is the beauty of it, for it allows one to be everywhere and at one point without being attached or detached from either.

Thus, the transonically omnipresent Word that flows through the core of one's being in God is also the Light of the world.

It is the solar Consciousness that is a Light unto Itself in the temple of God, the body of man, woman, and child.

It is by rejecting the Christ or solar Consciousness of one's being that one becomes bound to the worlds of duality.

However, as the solar Consciousness is ever a part of one's consciousness in God, Salvation is ever right at the door of consciousness.

Thus, the solar or Christ Consciousness is the door or way out of the bondage of duality. It is the Christ within you that is the way, the truth, the life, and the door, which is why there can be no other way.

To see the Christ as the Christ is, is to see yourself as you are, which is to realize you are the way that God had provided for you; for the way is the Word, the Christ within you.

Thus, the way is a created part of one's being in God. Any other imaginable way would only lead to failure. The way of the Word of God is not subject to failure.

Once one catches the returning ray of the Word of God, there is nothing that can stop or hinder one from returning to the Christ of one's being in God.

The way of the Word of God is based on the cause and effect relationship of it, and the cause and effect are two parts of the same thing in the way of God.

The way back to God is assured for all who desire to return to God, for it is built into the nature of one's being in God.

One cannot get away from God by pretending God does not exist, or by trying to move away from God; for what exists does so in relation to God, and all directions are within the Being of God.

The going-away ray reverses itself and becomes the returning ray. It is a matter of whether one is conscious or unconscious of going out and returning. It is just that the returning ray of the Word of God is always there for one to catch for the return home.

It's not a matter of all souls moving in the same direction at the same time as far as appearances go. It is just that all directions are a part of one direction.

It is the two-way motion of the one direction that allows one to move back and forth through the many mansions within the one world without end.

It is the two-way motion of the Word of God that allows one to go into the inner worlds of the solar Consciousness and then return to the worlds of duality to lend assistance to those who are ready for the returning ray.

If one is taken out of the body in the sleep state and experiences the Christ Consciousness, it is as though the coming were as a thief in the night.

Even if one were to remember the experience upon awakening, which may or may not be, since it could be a conscious or an unconscious thing, it appears as a thief in the night to all others.

The second coming, or the returning to the Christ Consciousness is ever a personal thing. However, it is a universal thing, for who is to say how many the Christ of one may awaken the Christ in others of the one universal Christ?

That is, to see the Christ within another is to see the Christ within oneself, and thus become like unto the Christ. Thus, who is to say how many realize the Christ at any one time in the history of the world?

As the solar or Christ Consciousness is the neutronic central Consciousness of one's being in God, those of the Christ Consciousness many well refer to themselves as Neutronians while dwelling in the worlds of duality.

CHAPTER FIVE

The Transonic Worlds

Inasmuch as all worlds are included in the one world that is without end, we can refer to the one world as a Transonic world. We need a means of expression that transcends expression without doing it.

Thus, if we can come to realize that a Transonic thing is a threefold thing wherein each part is interchangeable with the others, we can develop a means of expression to express the inexpressible.

Once we realize how the parts of a threefold thing are interchangeable, we come to realize that they are interchangeable without being interchangeable, for each part is the other part without being the other part. We realize that to be the nature of a Transonic thing, which contains a description without containing one.

As we realize the Transonic interaction of threefold things, we can realize that a threefold thing is not the end of all things.

As the parts of a threefold thing are transonically linked together in such a way that the parts come not together or apart, the threefold whole of a thing is realized to be a part of another threefold whole that has become a part of a greater whole.

Accordingly, parts are transonically linked together to Transonic infinity, and wholes are transonically linked together to Transonic infinity; for parts and wholes exist in relation to one another.

By absorbing the nature of a Transonic thing into consciousness, we are absorbing the Consciousness of all things.

A Transonic thing is that which has neither beginning nor end. Thus, a Transonic thing is both before and after itself, yet at the center without being in any of these places.

That which can be this, that, and the other thing, without being anything, is that which is everything and no-thing in the All-Oneness of Being, the Transonic Consciousness.

The Transonic Word is that which can break both the silent and the sound barrier within Itself, for It is both silence and sound without being either.

Once we see that a Transonic thing represents all things, not just any one thing, and that the sound or the Word of God represents all things, we can keep the word sound in relation to the word *Transonic*.

As the Word or the Sound of God contains all things within and without Itself, the Sound or Word is Transonic, which is to say that the Sound breaks the barrier of Itself to Transonic infinity.

It is just that Transonic Sound includes, not only the silence within it, but all things, and is therefore not what it might appear to be.

Transonic power, light, love, wisdom, spirit, freedom, and so on are all a Transonic part of the Transonic Sound or Word of God.

As far as appearances go, one can hear and feel and move with the Sound Current. Although the Sound Current is heard and felt differently on different planes of being, I recall moving within what seems to be the sound of a rushing wind, and felt the wind on my body.

There were also experiences of moving without the sound of wind. There is also the experience of moving backward into the past. There is also the experience of moving up and back through what appears as worlds of solid matter.

Your experiences may not be as another, for there are many to be had in the inner worlds. It is just that all experiences are possible to all. It is through one's own experiences that one receives the lessons suitable for one at any given time.

To get back to the concept of what a Transonic world is, in case you haven't come to your own conclusion by now, let us go back to the concept of the dual world or the world of duality. We can see that what we can call electronians and protonians are dwelling in the worlds of duality. We can also see how that what we can call neutronians can also dwell there.

Thus, by extension, we can see that the electronians, the protonians, and the neutronians are all transonians appearing as one or the other.

It is a matter of what awareness one has in relation to the All-Oneness of the Transonic Consciousness.

Accordingly, the electronians, the protonians, the neutronians, and the transonians all dwell in what appears as the world of duality, for some are in the world, yet not of it.

It is when neutronians predominate that the planetary body undergoes the process of its Salvation consciously, for it is the neutronians that reconcile the opposites of conflict through the core of being, the Christ Self, unto God; for that is what restores the people of a planet, and the planet itself back to God.

The Transonic Word interpenetrates all worlds within the one world without end. The Transonic Consciousness is the Consciousness that penetrates the consciousness of all things. The Transonic Consciousness is the Consciousness that moves away and toward Itself, carrying all with It.

Thus, the Transonic Consciousness is the Consciousness of the Word of God. The Word of God is that Consciousness. It is the Transonic Consciousness that flows through the neutronian consciousness into all worlds.

Just as one may become bound to a positive or negative consciousness, one may also become bound to the solar consciousness, for the solar consciousness is bound to a solar system until the solar consciousness becomes Transonic.

There are many solar systems within the one solar system within the one world within many of the one world without end.

It is a matter of overcoming one solar system before even thinking of moving to another consciously.

As one solar system is transonically linked to another to Transonic infinity, it is not so much a problem of how to move from one to another, for one does that unconsciously before learning to do it consciously.

Thus, no matter what one might do that would at first appear astounding is not really that astounding when it takes place, for it is as though one were already doing it in the first place.

Even though one may not be aware of going out of the body while in the sleep state, one does so, which is doing what one wouldn't believe one could do in the first place.

One is doing the seemingly impossible all the time without knowing it being done. Anyway, when one leaves the body in so-called death, one goes to where one has been going while in the sleep state.

When one comes face to face with what one is doing, it doesn't appear so great. The little things are just as great as the big things in the Transonic Consciousness of God. There is one thing that would, from one frame of reference, appear to be a great thing, if not an impossible thing, not that this thing is any different from any other thing.

What we are referring to here is the finding of one's soul mate, and uniting with it in the solar consciousness of one's being on the soul plane. Usually, when we read about this while in the physical body, we are left with an emptiness as to what it really is that is supposed to take place.

It's not so much a matter of explaining it to someone else, but one of explaining it to oneself. That is, when one is on an inner soul plane where one can see things happening right before one's eyes, one is still left with the thought as to how one does that.

Just as one comes to know without knowing, one comes to do without doing in the Consciousness of God. Thus, it's not a matter knowing how to unite with one's soul mate. It just happens whether one knows the how of it or not.

CHAPTER SIX

The World Set in the Heart

Until one becomes conscious of the nature of one's creation in God, and is consciously present at the creation, the world is, as it were, set in the heart; and there's no way of finding out how that might be.

It's not really a mystery, for the world is set in the heart of us all whether it is realized or not; for the worlds of the one world are a part of the being of us all, who are created in the Being of God.

The reason that the world is set in the heart without one realizing how, when, where, or why is that the world has neither end nor beginning as it would appear to the one unaware of the nature of creation.

To determine how it is that the world is set in the heart, and the nature of creation, one must see things as they have always been, as they are, and as they shall ever be in the everlasting Consciousness of God.

To transcend the ignorance of not knowing the nature of creation, one need only realize that, as one is part of the creation of God, one already knows the nature of creation, but is unaware of that Transonic fact.

Again, it is no mystery that one can be unaware of that which one is already aware, for awareness and unawareness are a part of one's beginningless and endless nature in the Being of God.

One can come to the realization in the nature of one's being in God that all things are the same today, yesterday, and forever. That is, one can come to realize that the seeming changes within the nature of being are but a part of the sameness of it.

It is ever true that there is nothing new under the sun. It is ever a matter of becoming aware of what already is in the Consciousness of God, which is the Consciousness of all things, for God is the All in All of Being.

Things appear mysterious, complicated, and impossible, but things are never as they appear to be. Thus, the seemingly impossible is not impossible, but only appears to be.

The seemingly impossible nature of creation is not only in the realm of the possible, but is a natural part of the nature of one's consciousness in the Consciousness of God. It is a matter of becoming conscious of what one is doing unconsciously anyway.

Thus, becoming conscious of the nature of creation does not change the nature of it. It is just the unconscious becoming conscious.

The world is set in the heart both consciously and unconsciously. Thus, the unconscious becomes conscious, and the conscious becomes unconscious because neither has a beginning or end.

It's a matter of becoming aware of the conscious and unconscious interaction within the nature of being, and of reconciling the conscious with the unconscious.

Consciousness is Transonic, which is to say that it is linked to unconsciousness as parts of the same thing. The nature of consciousness is such that the conscious and the unconscious reverse from one to the other to Transonic infinity as a part of the same function.

The nature of all things created in the Consciousness of God is created as threefold parts of one thing. Thus, the reversal from one thing to another is but a change within the unchangeable nature of the one thing.

Accordingly, what appears as the cycle of birth and death, the one reversing to the other, is but a part of the nature of life and death. The one becomes the other because it is ever hidden in the other.

Likewise, the one world without end has within it the potential of becoming another world to Transonic infinity. Thus, there is an infinity of worlds within the one world because of the endless and beginningless nature of it.

Inasmuch as nothing really changes within the nature of one's creation, there is always a sense in which one is in control of one's creation, for one is created in both awareness and unawareness as parts of the same thing.

By becoming aware of the nature of creation, one becomes aware of how one brings destruction on oneself without knowing how, when, where, or why one does so.

By becoming aware of the nature of creation, one becomes aware that creation and destruction are parts of the same thing; and can thereby take conscious control of creation and avoid any unwanted destruction.

That is, both creation and destruction are built into the nature of one's creation in God, and therefore neither are what they might appear to be.

Just as life and death interact and reverse from one to the other while remaining the same thing, creation and destruction interact and reverse from one to the other while remaining the same thing.

To be conscious of creation is to be conscious that there is no such thing as destruction as it would appear, for destruction is but a part of the process of creation, and vice versa.

One overcomes the destruction that appears to be by becoming conscious of what the creation is in the Transonic Consciousness of God.

Thus, there is no escape from the destruction that is an essential part of the creation of God. However, by reconciling creation and destruction through the living Christ of Being unto God, one overcomes both creation and destruction within the nature of one's being in God.

To see death as a Transonic thing, which is to see it as a Transonic part of life, is to bring immortality to the Light of consciousness, for there is no immortality that excludes the Transonic death that is an essential part of Transonic life.

Creation and destruction are Transonic parts of the same thing because neither creation nor destruction has a beginning or end as it would appear they should have.

The point I am trying to get to is to somehow explain how it is that when one is in the dream world within the worlds of one's being, worlds appear and disappear without one knowing how that might be.

The nature of the many worlds within the one world is such that to become unconscious of one world or situation is to become aware of another world or situation.

It is the nature of one's creation to have the ability to make the transfers from one world to another. However, one is not necessarily conscious of having that ability, for one must incorporate the seemingly unconscious into the nature of consciousness in order to be conscious of having conscious control of one's creation.

In order words, creation is a Transonic thing, for it is also Transonic destruction. Thus, the Consciousness that creates destruction as a part of creation is the Transonic Consciousness of God that is without beginning or end.

Therefore, one must become conscious in a Transonic way, which is to make the unconscious a part of one's conscious awareness in order to be aware of making the transfer from one world or situation to another in both the outer or inner worlds of one's being in God.

It is as though there are an infinite number of worlds or situations to choose from within the inner worlds of one's being. And one is making the choices whether it be consciously or unconsciously, for such is the Transonic nature of the one world within another to Transonic infinity, the one world without end.

CHAPTER SEVEN

The Indestructible World

We are becoming aware that the one world of many that is without beginning or end is, indeed, an indestructible world. That is, we are finding that the seeming destructibility in the nature of creation is really what makes it indestructible in the first place.

We are learning that there is no such thing as destruction in the creation of God. As all seeming opposites do, creation and destruction exist in relation to one another.

That is, one part of an opposite is the Transonic cancellation of the other. The one cancels the other without doing it, for the one is a Transonic part of the other.

The seeming creation and destruction of a thing is but the one thing participating in the process of multiplying Itself to Transonic infinity.

By operating within the Transonic Consciousness of God, one becomes conscious of, not only the creation of oneself in God; but also the destruction of oneself in God, for the creation and the destruction are parts of one function.

By transcending the limited consciousness of seeing things as they appear to be, and entering the unlimited Consciousness that operates in accord with the nature of God, one is in conscious control of both creation and destruction; for then it is God within one that is in control.

The nature of creation is such that God must become, and perform all the functions within Itself, for God is the All in All.

As the All in All of Being, God is the highest and lowest; therefore, God operates within the lowest as well as the highest, for all things are but Transonic manifestations of God.

Accordingly, one can only appear to operate outside the Consciousness of God, for the seemingly outside is but a part of the inside of God.

No matter what one might think God might be, one must face the reality of what that is, one way or other, for one exists in relation to what that is.

One proves nothing by trying to deny God, or to run away from God, for there is no denying of God, and there is nowhere to go but to God; for there is no-thing that is not included in God.

Accordingly, one is not free until one consciously works in accord with the nature of God as God is in Transonic reality.

Freedom is, therefore, a Transonic thing. One can only have the freedom of God, whether it be conscious or unconscious freedom, for the freedom of God is all the freedom there can or need be; for God is all there is in Transonic reality.

One is free to the degree that one is operating in accord with the nature of God, which is the nature of one's being in God.

Accordingly, the freedom of God is the freedom in God, and is not freedom as it would appear to the mind of duality, for the freedom of God is not something separate from bondage.

That is, so-called freedom and bondage function as parts of the same thing in the Consciousness that has transcended duality.

Accordingly, there are bounds or limitations set upon the freedom of God; however, they are the limitations that God set upon Itself because of the nature of God, which is without beginning or end.

Thus, one can have the Transonic freedom of God by operating in accord with the Consciousness of God. The freedom of God is not realized by the mind of duality, for duality is a boundary God sets around the freedom of Itself.

Therefore, one must go through the strait gate, as it were, the narrow way, the core of being, the Christ Self, and thereby reconcile the opposites of duality in order to realize what the freedom of God might be.

There is, as it were, a gulf fixed between the worlds of duality and the realm of the Christ Consciousness, for one must overcome the worlds of duality in order to enter the realms beyond the worlds of duality.

No matter how one might express it, the way to God is guarded on all sides, for it is because of the nature of one's being in God that makes things be that way.

That is, God sets bounds around the realm of Itself until It can operate within the balanced nature of Itself. Thus, God doesn't operate somewhere off apart from creation, but experiences the worlds of creation just as all things do.

God becomes what you are in order for you to become what God is. God becomes as you because God is a Transonic part and whole of your and you become as God because you are a Transonic part and whole of God.

God sets limitations upon Itself in that It cannot separate Itself from you; and, of course, you being a Transonic part and whole of God cannot separate yourself from God. That is the boundary set on your freedom in God.

That is, you cannot free yourself from God because you are transonically linked to God. You are, therefore, free without being free, for your only freedom is the freedom you have in God.

Accordingly, to move through the indestructible worlds of the inner planes of one's being in God, one must conform to the way of doing it in accord with the nature of God.

However, there are many ways of moving within the inner planes of being, but all ways are a part of the motion in the Being of God. That is, there is motion in relation to the worlds of duality, and there is motion that relates itself differently beyond the worlds of duality.

In the higher inner worlds, there is not only horizontal movement, but there is vertical movement from a world below to above, and vice versa.

One can also go from one inner world to one above in the same manner one leaves the physical body in the sleep state and goes into the inner worlds.

That is, one could leave the inner body and go to a higher world. However, what impresses itself on me the most is the conscious movement of the body from a lower to a higher world and the movement back.

For in moving is such a way, one gets the impression of moving through what appears as solid matter. While one is moving is such a way, the body changes to be in accord with the vibrations of whatever plane it enters, but the consciousness is the same on all planes of being.

Thus, one comes to learn through experience that spirit and matter function as two parts of the same thing. One comes to realize that one is Transonic spirit, which is also Transonic matter.

The worlds are found to be indestructible because spirit and matter are found to be transonically the same thing. Thus, spirit becomes matter and matter becomes spirit as one moves from one world to another.

Thus, as one world disappears, another world appears. One world appears to be uncreated and another world appears to be created; yet neither take place, for both worlds exist as one in the other as parts of the same thing.

It is within the realm of the Christ Consciousness, which is beyond duality, without being beyond it, that one realizes the indestructibility of the one world without end, for one must have reconciled spirit and matter before entering the Christ Consciousness where spirit and matter function as parts of the same thing.

CHAPTER EIGHT

The Macrocosmic World

Perhaps, by now we can begin to realize that the macrocosmic world is none other than the one world without end that we are and have been considering.

That is, the macrocosmic world need not be some vague concept within the mind, for it is the Transonic Body of God in which we all live, move, and have being.

Inasmuch as the macrocosmic world is the Body of God, it is also our body of man, for our body of is the temple of God. We are a part of the macrocosmic world of God because we are a part of the infinite Being of God.

Accordingly, we operate within the confines of the Body of God whether it is realized or not, for one does so unconsciously until one learns to do so consciously.

Thus, the macrocosmic world can become a part of one's consciousness in God, for one is already a part of the Consciousness of God.

The macrocosmic world can be integrated into one's seemingly finite consciousness because the macrocosmic world is a Transonic part of the microcosmic world of one's being in God.

That is, the macrocosmic world and the microcosmic world are transonically the same thing in the Consciousness of God, for they are transonically linked together in such a way that they neither come together nor apart.

The whole of God and the part of God are one hidden in the other, for all things of God are hidden within themselves. That is, they are transonically hidden, which is to say they are hidden without being hidden.

One must transcend, without doing so, both the simplicity and the complexity of one's being in God in order to operate in accord with the modus operandi of the Consciousness of God.

In that one is a part of the All in All of God, one must surrender the part of being that one may think is separate from God in order to function consciously within the All in All of God.

As one is a Transonic part of God, surrendering to God is surrendering to the Transonic Self of one's being in God.

Thus, by surrendering one's microcosmic self, one unites it to one's macrocosmic Self, and one thereby becomes the instrument of the All in All in the one world without end.

The macrocosmic Self surrenders Itself to the microcosmic self just as the microcosmic self surrenders to the macrocosmic Self.

Therefore, the modus operandi of both selves is the same, for the Self of selves is the one Transonic Self. One can picture the Transonic interaction of the macrocosmic and the microcosmic parts of being even though one has not experienced the interaction.

That is, when the little self rises up through the inner planes of being, it takes on the higher vibrations of the higher planes and becomes the higher part of Self.

No matter how high one might go on the ladder of God, even unto the formless Body of God, one becomes the higher body as one ascends to the higher. Thus, little self realizes that it is the great Self.

Conversely, the macrocosmic or great Self takes on the vibrations of the lower planes of being as It descends to the physical world. Thus, the macrocosmic Self comes to realize that It is also the microcosmic self.

There is nowhere the little self and the great Self can come together or apart, for they are transonically the same thing. The Transonic Self includes the macrocosmic and the microcosmic self, for It is the Transonic reconciliation of all things within and without Itself.

The Transonic Word of God is that which links all things together as one Transonic thing. The Transonic Word of God links all things from atoms to the universe.

All things are ever in their rightful places in all universes of God, for all things move in accord with the Transonic pattern of creation.

Thus, if one does not consciously balance the creation within oneself, the creation will balance itself anyway by means of built in self-destruction.

There is no point in denying the self-destruction built into the unbalanced creations of one's thoughts, for you need only think back or look around you for such evidence.

One way or the other, we are operating within the context of that which is without beginning or end, the one world without end. Thus, by going against the nature of one's being in God by refusing to surrender the little self to the great Self, and vice versa, one is only delaying what, by nature of one's being in God, must take place.

Accordingly, all do eventually bow to the Transonic Self of the chosen one of God, for as in all things, one is doing that unconsciously whether one knows it or not. Besides, one eventually realizes that one is bowing to that which is a Transonic part of one's being in God.

The Transonic purpose of the messenger of the Transonic Word of God is to link the little self to the great Self in order for the Self to realize that it is the Transonic Self of God, the All in All.

Inasmuch as one is linked to the Transonic Word, whether it is realized or not, the linkage is not some complicated thing as it might appear.

As the Transonic Word of God links all things, It is omnipresent throughout all worlds within the one world without end. Attempts to describe what the Transonic Word might be may either help or confuse one.

Thus, the Word may be referred to as the voice of God, the sound current of God, the spirit, the love, or as a wave going out and returning to itself.

It is by means of the Transonic Word that the little self can travel through the inner planes to the great Self back again to the little self.

The wave, if you call it that, is going in both directions at the same time. Therefore, one can always reverse directions and return to God by means of the Transonic Word that is a Transonic part of oneself.

When one sees the Word as It is, which is seeing the Christ as It is, one links oneself to the Transonic Word that leads one back to the God realm, which is all a part of seeing the living Christ as the Christ is, and becoming like unto the Christ.

Inasmuch as the Word of God appears to be going in two directions, which is really a part of the one direction, there is one, the spiritual part, that ever seeks to deliver one from the lower posio-negative worlds.

However, as the same time, the posio-negative part of the wave of God ever seeks to trap one in the posio-negative worlds. Such is the conflict of the spirit and the flesh, as it were. The solution to the conflict is in reconciling the two functions of the wave of the Word of God, and let the wolf and lamb of being, as it were, the positive and the negative dwell together in Transonic harmony by reconciling all things through the living Christ Self unto God so that God may be consciously realized to be the All in All of one's being.

CHAPTER NINE

The Absolute World

Once we come to realize the Transonic nature of the one world without end, which includes all worlds within and without the Consciousness of God, we realize that we cannot describe the world simply as being absolute, for that implies a limit that one doesn't want to imply.

Just as the one world is not what it appears to be because of the Transonic nature of it, the limitations of the absolute are not what they appear to be.

That is, the absolute is not limited to being absolute, but is limited in that it cannot exist apart from the relative part of itself.

The absolute and the relative are Transonic parts of the same thing, not something separate from one another.

The absolute nature of God, which includes the nature of all things, is indescribable, for it cannot be described apart from the relative nature of God.

Consequently, the absolute cannot be experienced apart from the relative, and vice versa. Thus, we come to realize that there is no such thing as the absolute apart from the relative, for that would be a kingdom divided against itself.

Accordingly, there is neither the absolute nor the relative as it would appear to the mind that sees in relation to duality.

Just as life and death are Transonic parts of the same thing, the absolute and the relative are Transonic parts of the same thing.

Just as the Kingdom of God is within, which includes the without, the one world without end is within and without one's consciousness in God.

Thus, the absolute and the relative are both a part of one's consciousness in God. Thus, one cannot be expected to understand either the absolute or the relative without experiencing it within one's own consciousness in God.

Inasmuch as the absolute and the relative are both a part of one's consciousness in God, one can come to understand them by doing so in accord with the nature of what they are in Transonic reality, for one is a Transonic being whether it is realized or not.

One comes to realize the nature of one's being in God by means of experiencing both the seeming relative and the seeming absolute parts of one's being in the Consciousness of God.

Just as one experiences death while calling it life, one experiences the relative while calling it the absolute. Just as one calls death, life, one calls the relative, the absolute. Thus, overcoming the relative is overcoming the absolute, for the one is hidden in the other.

Each world appears as absolute until one gets above it, and then the world above appears as absolute, and the lower world appears as relative.

Accordingly, as one moves from a lower to a higher world, the absolute and the relative interchange positions, just as life and death interchange positions, for just as life and death, the relative and the absolute are transonically the same thing.

Thus, one could move forever from a lower to a higher world and never find the absolute as something separate from the relative.

However, by going into the higher world within one's being in God, one comes to realize the Transonic nature of the absolute, and returns with that information.

The absolute consciousness is not the end of itself, for it is a Transonic part of that which is before and after itself, the Transonic Consciousness.

Accordingly, both the absolute and the relative are without beginning or end. The one can and does perform the function of the other, for that is the nature of their creation in the Consciousness of God.

Therefore, the absolute and the relative are but seeming opposites that are to be reconciled through the living Christ unto God so that God may be realized to be what God is in Transonic reality.

Accordingly, the absolute and the relative, as well as all seeming opposites, are transonically linked through the living Christ Self at the core of one's being in God.

It is within the Christ Consciousness that one realizes why it is that there is neither male nor female, positive nor negative, absolute nor relative, for the opposites are reconciled through the Christ Consciousness.

By reconciling the absolute with the relative, one is but realizing what they are in Transonic reality.

By reconciling what appears as absolute spirit with what appears as absolute matter, one is reconciling all worlds within the one world without end.

It is the through the Christ Self at the core of being that the balance of opposites is maintained. It is through the Christ Self that all things are delivered unto God, for the Christ is that which represents the reconciliation of all opposites within Itself.

It is the Christ Self that delivers all unto God, for it is the Christ Self that realizes that God is the All in All whether realized or not.

Inasmuch as the Christ Self is the Transonic reconciliation of all things within and without itself, it is the Christ Self that is in position to give all up unto God.

Although the sacrifice of the Christ Consciousness cannot be simply what it might appear to be, one is not in position to make the sacrifice consciously until one has realized the Christ Consciousness.

The sacrifice of Christ is on behalf of Itself in that the sacrifice is a part of the nature of all things in the Consciousness of God.

However, in that all things are included in the Christ Consciousness, the sacrifice of Christ is on behalf of all, for it reveals the nature of the sacrifice to be a part of one's being in God, not simply as a substitute for another.

However, by viewing the sacrifice as a substitute, one gets the benefits of that until the nature of the wholeness of it is revealed to one's consciousness in God.

That is, one makes the sacrifice within the being of God unconsciously until one is prepared to do so consciously.

It is by making the sacrifice of giving all, that one receives all, for one cannot realize what all is until one consciously makes the sacrifice.

Thus, the sacrifice of Christ is not the sacrifice of any given body, but the whole body of God. That is, it is the sacrifice of everything in the Consciousness of God, for it is the giving of all; for the nature of God is such that the giving of all is the receiving of all, and vice versa.

It is the giving up of the Christ Self, at the core of being, that the Christ Self is realized to be the Transonic Self, and not what It might appear to be.

That is, the Christ Self comes to realize that It is a Self within a Self to Transonic infinity, just as there is a world within a world to Transonic infinity.

The Transonic Self is the Transonic goal of all who travel any path to God whether realized or not, for there is no rest from searching until one reaches the goal of goals, and finds that there is nothing to be found by searching, for one must realize how it is that nothing is lost before one can cease searching for the unsearchable.

CHAPTER TEN

The Transonic Wedding

As we realize that the many worlds are linked together as one world without end, we come to the realization of the Transonic wedding.

It is because of the Transonic linkage of the one world in many that we can realize that we are in the world, yet not in it.

We need to realize the whole as well as the part in order to avoid becoming bound to any one world.

Each world within the one world without end appears to be a separate world, but the separation is a Transonic one. That is, the worlds do not come together, and they do not come apart. They are together without being together, and they are apart without being apart, transonically.

It is because of the Transonic linkage of the worlds that allows one to travel up and back through the worlds. Thus, as one moves from a lower world to a higher, the lower gives way to the higher; and as one moves from a higher to a lower world, the higher gives way to the lower.

Accordingly, the worlds interchange with one another. The lower becomes the higher, and the higher becomes the lower.

As the worlds are Transonic worlds, they are made up of interchangeable spirit and matter. That is, the spirit and the matter of one world is the spirit and the matter of all the worlds within the one world without end.

As one moves through the inner worlds of one's being, spirit and matter interchange as one moves through them. Therefore, from one frame of reference, it would appear that one were moving through matter.

The point to be made is that spirit and matter are transonically the same thing, which is to say they are the same thing without being the same thing.

Accordingly, spirit and matter are wedded together transonically from one world to another to Transonic infinity, just as the worlds are transonically wedded together to Transonic infinity.

Thus, the Soul, the Self that moves through the worlds takes on the spirit and matter of the worlds It dwells on, or passes through.

Thus, the Soul or the Self of one's being is Transonic, for It can move from one body or world to another and back again, for It is not attached to any body or world.

By the time one has realized that the world is a world without end, one has realized that one's consciousness is without beginning or end.

It is the consciousness that transcends both the beginning and the end of itself that takes on the All in All of Consciousness.

That is, by giving up all, one comes to realize that Consciousness is Transonic, for by giving all, one receives all back transonically.

One comes to realize that all things are linked together as the many in one within one's Transonic Consciousness.

Accordingly, one possess all by not possessing anything. To simply possess something is to seem to have, which is to have that eventually taken away.

A Transonic thing cannot be taken away or destroyed. That is, having and not having, creation and destruction are Transonic parts of the same thing, which is what is in Transonic reality.

Once we realize that the pattern of one thing is as the pattern of all things, we realize that all things in the universe of universes are transonically wedded together whether it is realized or not.

That is, nature is not really going to change; for, as all things, it is the same today, yesterday, and forever; for it is as the nature of the Transonic Creator of it.

Therefore, what we are ever doing is becoming aware of what already is. That is, we can become conscious of parts of being that we were unconscious of before.

It is the conscious and the unconscious interacting within themselves that makes the unchangeable appear to change.

Thus, the changeable and the unchangeable are not separate things, for they are transonically wedded together as one; and are, therefore, interchangeable parts of the same thing.

Accordingly, the number of bodies that Soul could appear in is infinite, for the one body is interchangeable with all bodies; yet the Consciousness within the bodies is always the same no matter what body It may assume.

Thus, the body is Transonic, not just one but one in many as well as many in one. It is because the Soul is the same apart from the body It appears in, that the Soul of one body can occupy the same space as the Soul within another body.

Thus, Soul can dwell within any number of bodies without feeling any change within the nature of Itself.

As is the nature of all things, Soul is a Transonic thing, for It is one in many to Transonic infinity. That is, Soul or Self is a Transonic multiple of Itself to Transonic infinity.

It is because the Soul or Self can occupy the space of another, that to see the Christ in another is to see the Christ in oneself, which is to realize what one really is, was, and will be in the first place.

The Christ is always with you because the Soul or Self of Christ is the Soul or Self of another. It is a matter of becoming aware of what already is in Transonic reality. That is, to see the Christ as the Christ is in Transonic reality is to see yourself as you are in Transonic reality.

If we can absorb into consciousness the essence of what a Transonic thing is, we can picture what a Transonic wedding of a man and woman might be.

That is, a Transonic wedding must be a wedding without being one, for it weds without wedding, for the wedding is one within one to Transonic infinity. In the Transonic wedding, things come neither together nor apart.

Thus, for man and woman to arrive at the point of the Transonic wedding, each has to individually arrive there at the same point where Consciousness is realized to be Transonic. That is, each realizes that the wedding is not just of one plane of being, and that it includes all planes of being in the Consciousness of God.

Thus, from the highest to the lowest, and vice versa, Transonic man and Transonic woman would have an agreement that is also Transonic, form one world to another.

Transonic man and Transonic woman have both transcended the body-consciousness to realize that the one body is one in many and many in one.

Therefore, both Transonic man and Transonic woman come to realize that it is not just the body that is the mate that one is ever searching for, but that which indwells it.

Thus, the Soul of both Transonic man and Transonic woman have the ability to appear in any number of bodies, for Soul can appear in any number of bodies.

It is as though all bodies are eliminated as choices before one finds one's Transonic Mate. That is, as in all things, one must lose something before one can find it as it is in Transonic reality, for losing and finding are transonically the same thing in Transonic Consciousness.

One's Transonic mate is always with one, for as one moves from one body to another, one's Transonic mate does too, for It is ever a part of one's Transonic Consciousness.

That is, at all levels of consciousness, one is the potential mate of another at that level of consciousness.

CHAPTER ELEVEN

The Transonic Wedding 2

That is, from the level of the mineral, plant, and animal to the human, Christ, and God Consciousness, Transonic mates are growing together.

Accordingly, everything is a potential, Transonic mate to every other thing. Therefore, we are beginning to realize that the mate that one is seeking is not one mate, but the one mate that is one in many and many in one, the Transonic mate.

Therefore, at whatever level of awareness that one may be at, one's Transonic mate is there also, for it is a cause effect relationship. The male cannot be separated from the female, and vice versa, for it's a part of the one Consciousness in the first place.

Thus, one's Transonic mate is not a particular mate, but the mate of mates, so to speak. That is, one's Transonic mate is one in many and many in one.

That is, the Transonic male represents the one in many and the many on one, and the Transonic female does also.

Therefore, the Transonic wedding of Transonic man and Transonic woman is the wedding of the male that is one in many and many in one with the female that is one in many and many in one.

However, before these things would even considered a possibility, both the male and the female will have reconciled the entire posio-negative universe in order to arrive at such a possibility.

That is, both male and female will have transcended, without doing so, both the male and the female, which are but parts of one's threefold being.

The Soul, the essential Self of one's being in God is transonically neutral. It is the Transonic neutron at the core of being, and is therefore neither male nor female, but can take on the appearance of one or the other.

Thus, Soul, being Transonic, has the potential of becoming trapped in the posio-negative marriage of the worlds of duality.

Therefore, it is up to both male and female as individuals to realize that, in Transonic reality, there is neither male nor female, in that they are appearances of the Soul or Self that dwells therein.

It is by reconciling the male and the female, the positive and the negative, the wolf and the lamb of one's being through the core of being, the Christ Self, unto God that one overcomes the worlds of duality, which is the realm of death that appears as life; for life and death are transonically the same thing. But the dual mind doesn't know that, and therefore becomes bound to an illusion of reality.

It is when one overcomes the worlds of duality that one enters the Christ Self at the core of being, the neutronic Self, which is Self-realization.

It is the sacrificing of the that Self--realization, or the giving up of it, that one is in position to realize what a Transonic thing might be.

That is, if one sees Self-realization as the end of all seeking, one becomes bound at that level of awareness until that level is also overcome, for there is no end to seeking, for it has no beginning in the first place.

Therefore, one must continue to overcome anything that appears to be an end to anything in order to reach finally that point where it is realized there is neither end nor beginning to anything.

Thus, Soul or Self must overcome the inclination to believe that It is a Soul separate from all other souls, for such belief leads to the possibility of setting oneself up as though one were God to the exclusion of something else; whereas, God, by nature of being that, must be the All in All, not something separate from that.

Thus, the Soul that thinks It, or anything else is separate from God, or that God is separate from anything is still in the process of becoming aware of what God is.

Therefore, the journey to God is not ended until one gets past the end, so to speak, for God is that which is both before and after Itself; for there is nowhere for God to begin or end.

Accordingly, there is no place for Soul or Self or the Christ to lay It's Head, as it were, once It realizes the Transonic nature of: Itself; for It moves within the context of that which is without beginning or end.

Thus, the Transonic Soul has gone beyond Itself to get to where It is, which is both before and after Itself.

As the Self may appear in the body of a male or female, It is neither one nor the other. Therefore, when the Self within the male body realizes its Transonic nature, It becomes Transonic, which is transonically one with the Self of all.

Accordingly, when the Self within the female body realizes its Transonic nature, It is the same Self realizing Its Transonic nature within the female body.

Thus, the Self of the male body is neither male nor female, and the Self of the female is neither male nor female.

Therefore, the one Self of selves is the Transonic mate to Itself to Transonic infinity, for it can divide Itself into both male and female to Transonic infinity.

The one Self individualizes Itself by dwelling within male and female bodies, and maintains that individuality after overcoming the body-consciousness.

It is just that the Transonic individuality of the Self is not personal to the exclusion of the impersonal. That is, the Transonic Self realizes that It is a cell in the whole, and that the part and the whole are as one transonically.

Therefore, when two seemingly separate Souls realize their Transonic nature, they still appear as one or the other.

Thus, to be transonically wedded to the whole is still to be wedded to the one that represents the whole.

As the Self takes on the appearance of the bodies of the world It dwells in, a Transonic Soul dwelling in the physical body would appear as any other.

To realize how two transonically realized Souls might meet upon the physical plane, both would have to have gone beyond themselves, as it were, and returned to where they were.

That is, while dwelling within the physical body, one may travel through the inner planes of being until one reaches the point of realizing there is neither end nor beginning to anything. One thereby links all things to the Consciousness that is from before the foundation of the world, as it were. By doing that, one returns to the physical body with the Transonic Consciousness.

Accordingly, if two Souls meet on the inner planes of being at the point of Transonic realization, they can link themselves together on each plane as they return to the physical body.

Therefore, it would be possible for two transonically realized Souls to meet on the physical plane of being, and from there realize that they are transonically linked together on all planes of being within the one world without end.

However, this is not to say that any two souls have met that way, for evidently, there are no records that would indicate that such a thing has taken place.

It is just that there is nothing that is impossible within the Consciousness of God, for the possible and the impossible are transonically the same thing in the Consciousness of God.

Perhaps such a thing is in the process of taking place, in that there is a cause and effect relationship to the possibility of it. That is, one cannot imagine something that does not exist already in one form or another.

CHAPTER TWELVE

The Instrument of God

The purpose of going away and returning to God is to realize God within one's consciousness in God. That is, the purpose of the creature is to find its Creator, and to realize what the Creator might be in relation to the creature.

Until one has realized God, the task at hand, and the purpose of being is to come to that realization, for God is all there is.

Thus, until one realizes that God is all there is, one still has a thirst for God that goes unsatisfied.

Although one must give up all in order to realize what God is in Transonic reality, the giving of all is found to be the receiving of all. Thus, it is something that one must experience within one's consciousness in God.

That is, the Consciousness of God cannot be realized or experienced apart from one's consciousness in God, for the Consciousness of God is Transonic, which is to say that It is the Consciousness of all that is, and all that is not.

Thus, one moves, and has being in God, whether one realizes it or not, for God is all there is whether one realizes it or not.

Therefore, what we are doing in becoming aware of God is becoming aware of what we are in God. We become conscious of out Transonic link to God.

As God is all there is, this, at first, seems to be more than one would even expect to get a grasp of within one's seemingly finite consciousness.

However, in the Consciousness of God, one thing can represent all things, for one thing and all things are transonically the same thing in Transonic reality.

Thus, the Transonic Word of God represents all things within and without the Consciousness of God. Therefore, the Word of God that is made flesh in the living Christ of the physical body represents the Word of God. Thus, the living Christ represents all there is in all the worlds of God within and without the one world without end.

Thus, the living Christ represents all within and without the everlasting Kingdom of God, for it is the living Christ that has gone into the inner mansions of being and returned to the physical body, making that body an instrument that links all things from the God realms of heaven above to the God realms of earth below.

Thus, the living Christ of the physical body has access to all the worlds within and without the Body of God. Thus, it is the living Christ that takes one into the Kingdom of God, for the living Christ delivers the kingdoms of the world unto the Kingdom of God.

The living Christ is, therefore, an instrument of God, a channel, a distributor of the Word of God, as a co-worker of God.

Inasmuch as the Christ dwells at the core of one's being in God, whether one knows it or not, one is a co-worker of the Christ of God whether one is conscious of it or not. We are just becoming conscious of what we are in God, for what we are in God doesn't change when we become conscious if it, for that is just becoming aware of what is already there in the unconscious.

As the Word of God represents all things in God, It represents all things seemingly outside of God, for the Word is as a wave going out and returning to God.

Thus, God includes both the inside and the outside of all things. The seeming two-way motion is transonically one motion, for one travels back and forth, to and from the inner and the outer mansions of being.

Thus, it is the physical body that represents all the bodies of the inner worlds of being, for it is transonically linked to all inner bodies.

Accordingly, the body of the living Christ is an instrument of the Word of God on all planes of being in all the worlds of God, for there is a body-instrument on each plane that corresponds to that plane of being.

The living Christ is the instrument of the energy, the power, the light, the love, and of all things of the Word of God.

The nature of the distribution of the things of God is such that what is returned to God is received back in exact proportion, which makes for the balancing of all things in the universe of God.

Thus, the judgment of Christ is not personal, for it allows one to determine it for oneself in accord with how one sees oneself as, or acts, or reacts to the Christ Consciousness, whether that be conscious or unconscious.

Thus, by seeing the Christ as is, one is seeing oneself as one is; and, therefore, receives accordingly, and becomes like unto the Christ, of which one was already like unto unconsciously.

Accordingly, one sees in oneself what one sees the Christ to be, and thereby receives from the Christ in exact proportion as is determined by God, and delivered through the instrument of the Word of God.

Thus, one can see the sense that underlies the saying that it is a fearful thing to fall into the hands of the living God. However, it need not be a fearful thing, for one has ever been receiving from God in exact proportion as the law of cause and effect determines.

It is just that one needs to come face to face with God, and realize how it is that one brings upon oneself whatever it might be that one experiences in the Consciousness of God.

That is, the living Christ is within one as the essential Self of one's being, for the Christ never really goes away. Thus, one receives through the instrument of the Christ, even though one may not realize there is such a thing as a Christ Self. It is by becoming aware that the Christ is there within as well as without that the Daystar is born in the heart of the people of God.

Thus, the Christ is born within one's consciousness, and not by means of the physical conception of birth, for the Christ is without beginning or end; therefore, without father or mother.

The Christ Self of all has ever been without beginning or end. It is just that the Daystar gives birth to itself within the conscious awareness that It is without beginning end.

The Christ Self becomes aware of what It is in the Consciousness of God, which is that which is the same, today, yesterday, and forever, before, as, and after Itself.

As the Christ gives birth to Itself in an individual, the individual becomes the co-worker of God, for the Christ of one and all is the co-worker of God.

Thus, the Christ of one is as the Christ of another. Therefore, all are destined to become co-workers of God, for one is that whether realized or not; for one is that at one level or the other in the realms of both the conscious and the unconscious.

Thus, one eventually prepares oneself to the point of awareness where one is attracted to the one of the living Christ Consciousness, and thereby comes to see the Christ as is, and oneself as one is, the co-worker of God.

One is, therefore, an instrument, a distributor, a channel of the Word of God to the degree that one is conscious of being that as a co-worker of God.

One becomes a co-worker of God, for one doesn't become God as though God were an end to something. Thus, God is not the end or beginning of anything as though one excluded the other. Therefore, God is the co-worker of Itself.

The whole and the parts of God are transonically the same thing. Thus, each cell in the Being of God is a co-worker of the whole of God.

CHAPTER THIRTEEN

The Instrument of God 2

As the Transonic Word represents all that is, and all that is not, the living Christ represents all that is, and all that is not. The living Christ is the universal instrument of God, and therefore represents all things in the Consciousness of God.

As the Self of the living Christ is transonically one with the essential Self of all things, the living Christ is omnipresent throughout the universes of God.

As the living Christ is not what It might appear to be, the omnipresence of the living Christ is not what it might appear to be, for the living Christ has transcended, without doing so, omnipresence itself.

That is, the individual body of the living Christ is transonically one with the universal Body of God.

The individuality and the universality of the living Christ is not what they might appear to be, for they are transonically the same thing within the All-Oneness of the Christ Consciousness.

It is by means of the universal aspect of the living Christ that the living Christ is in contact with all things in the universe, for all things in the universe are all transonically linked together. It's a matter of becoming aware of how that might be.

Thus, the individual body of the living Christ could be light years away from you, yet be right where you are, for from the point of reference of the living Christ, the Christ is where you are, for It dwells within your body where you are.

Thus, the Christ doesn't even have to travel to where you are to be where you are, for It is already there in the first place.

Therefore, the fact that one has the potential of operating within the context of omnipresence is not a complicated thing, for one is doing that unconsciously anyway.

It is just that omnipresence is a Transonic thing, not what it appears to be. Therefore, the living Christ is an instrument of the omnipresence of God because the living Christ has delivered omnipresence to God, and has received it back reconciled with one point.

The living Christ can transfer from one point to another and experience omnipresence that way. One could move from point to point to Transonic infinity, and never come to an end to oneself.

The individual Soul of Christ can move from one point to another, and be anywhere as an individual Soul. However, it still remains that the living Christ dwells within an infinite number of other individuals, which, can do the same thing within the context of their individuality.

Therefore, no matter how one wants to look at it, Transonic omnipresence is as real as anything can get, for it is what is, and cannot be anything else.

As all things operate within the context of the Transonic omnipresence of God, we all operate within the Transonic omnipresence of God. Thus, we need to determine where we are in relation to that omnipresence.

That is, one is an instrument of God at one level or the other, for there is nothing else to be an instrument in relation to other than God.

Thus, one may be at the level of being a negative instrument of God, which seeks to keeps souls trapped in worlds of duality. Or one may be a positive instrument of God, which seeks to raise the negative consciousness unto the positive consciousness.

Thus, those operating on the negative side of the wave of God are in conflict with those on the positive wave of God. Thus, the two-way motion of the wave of God appears to be in conflict with one another.

Therefore, the positive side of the wave cannot settle the conflict within itself, for it, unknowingly, excludes the negative part of itself.

It is, therefore, by means of the reconciliation of all things through the Christ Self unto God that the conflict is settled.

Thus, one may be an instrument of the reconciliation of the entire positive and negative universe. Thus, we have what we might call the electronic, the protonic, and the neutronic instruments of God, all of which are a part of the All-Oneness of God.

There is a certain amount of bondage related to any of the instruments, positive, negative, or neutral, if operating as separate instruments.

The neutronic instrument is free of the conflict of the positive and the negative parts of itself, for they are reconciled through the neutronic Christ Self. It is just that the neutronic self may become bound to itself.

The only thing that stands in the way of the freedom of the neutronic Self is the neutronic Self, itself. That is, the neutronic Christ Self must somehow get beyond Itself in order to realize the endless and beginningless nature of Itself.

It is when the threefold Christ Self loses Itself that It finds Itself as the Transonic Christ Self. It is the Transonic Christ Self that is from before the foundation of the world, for It is that which is without beginning or end.

Therefore, it is the Transonic instrument of the Word of God that consciously represents the Consciousness that is without beginning or end.

There is greater freedom of movement as one becomes more aware of what one is in the Consciousness of God. Transonic freedom is the greatest freedom, yet it is not freedom as freedom would appear to be, for freedom is transcended, without being so, in the Transonic Christ Consciousness.

The Transonic Christ Self is free of the trinity of Itself, for It has transcended that, without doing so, also. Thus, Transonic freedom is the freedom to operate within the universe of universes in accord with what freedom is in the Transonic Consciousness of God.

Thus, freedom is a Transonic thing, and not what it might appear to be. One is free to serve. That is, if there were such a thing as freedom as it would appear to be, then God would be free; yet God is the servant of all, for God is, as it were, the co-worker of Itself.

As the Transonic co-worker of God, one is free to choose the area of service one performs in relation to the All in All of God.

The transonically conscious co-worker of God is free in that there is no bondage associated with it, for so-called bondage and freedom are neutralized through the neutronic core of the Transonic Self.

The Consciousness of the Transonic Christ Self is as a two-way, Transonic motion in all directions within and without itself. It is transcendent in that it moves through and back through Itself, within Itself, yet beyond Itself.

The Transonic Self is as a two-way transducer that transfers power from one system to another. It is as a transformer that regulates the power of the Word from one world to another.

The Transonic Self is as a two-way transmitter of the Word of God. It is as a two-way translator of the Word of God as It moves through the worlds of God.

Therefore, whether conscious or unconscious, at one level or another, we are all distributors, channels, and co-workers of God. We are each the instrument of the Word of God at the level of awareness of the All-Oneness of God.

CHAPTER FOURTEEN

Strangers in the World

By absorbing the Transonic reality of the many worlds within the one world without end, we become open to the lessons the scriptures are trying to present.

We can now realize how it is that we are said to be strangers and pilgrims in the worlds of conflict, and that our citizenship is in the heavenly worlds beyond the worlds of conflict.

We now realize how that it is not only probable, but inevitable that the Lord of one's being returns to gather one up to where one's body in united, fashioned like unto the glorious body of the Lord.

We can now understand how that many of the historical past were not able to bear the revelation as to what the Christ is, for we now see that there is a progressive revelation as to what the Christ is.

Thus, those who have the hope, the expectation, and the love for the appearing of the Lord can have the appearing brought to the Transonic reality, the Transonic Light of one's consciousness, for by seeing the Lord as is, one realizes one's Transonic likeness in the Lord.

It's a matter of determining how it is that one becomes like unto the Christ. One becomes like unto the Christ because one is ever like unto the Christ whether one is conscious of it or not.

Thus, the one of the living Christ Consciousness can reveal the Christ Consciousness to another, for when another can see the Christ within the one of the living Christ Consciousness, the Christ Consciousness is transferred to the one who sees the Christ as is.

That is, the Christ of one awakens the Christ within another, which becomes the resurrection of the dead, the resurrection from the worlds of conflict, the worlds of duality.

The Christ Consciousness is the reconciliation of the opposites of one's being, of which the wolf and the lamb represent.

Therefore, the Christ Consciousness lifts one up and out of the worlds of conflict to where the Transonic oneness of all things is realized.

That is, the living Christ of the physical body and the universal Christ are the same thing. The Christ within one is the Christ within another.

Thus, each individual manifestation of the Christ is a manifestation of the universal Christ. The whole and the part are realized to be the same thing.

Thus, each individual within the Christ Consciousness represents, and is a co-worker of the universal Christ, for the individual and the universal Christ are transonically the same thing.

The living Christ, therefore, represents all things within and without the universe of universes, for all things are included within and without the universal Christ.

Accordingly, the living Christ of the physical body represents all who have, and all who have not realized the Christ Consciousness. All who have realized the Christ Consciousness, and have left the physical body represent, and support the one of the living Christ Consciousness of the physical body.

Therefore, although the entire burden of the universe falls upon the one of the living Christ Consciousness, the burden is shared by all within the universal Christ Consciousness of God.

Accordingly, on all levels of awareness within the Consciousness of God, one bears one's own burden; yet it is shared by all at that level.

Thus, the nature of being is such that one must bear the burden alone, yet share it. Inasmuch as one both bears and shares the burden of all things, we come to realize that there is no burden as it would appear to be, for the burden is actually lifted away within the living Christ Consciousness.

That is, burden and non-burden are realized to be transonically the same thing within the universal Christ Consciousness, for they are reconciled there.

Accordingly, it is the purpose of one's creation in God to eventually share the burden of all things, for each has the innate ability to do just that.

The ability to bear the burden of all is not realized to be necessary, or realized to be possible until one gives up all things, for when one gives up all things, one gives up the burden also.

By giving up the burden, one receives it back with the realization that it is shared by all, and that it is shared by none, in that the burden is canceled by nature of what it is in the Consciousness of God.

Therefore, no matter how much of a burden one may be called upon to bear, it is no more than one can bear at any given time, for one need not take upon oneself more that one can bear at any given time.

No matter where one may be on the ladder of consciousness, one has been guided and helped along the way, and is being helped along the way, for sharing and helping one another is the nature of what all things are in the Christ Consciousness of God, for it is so whether realized or not.

Therefore, realizing the Christ Consciousness, and overcoming the worlds of duality, the worlds of conflict, need not be projected off to some nonexistent future; for it can only be realized in the now, which includes both the past and the future.

The preparation of the past is but a preparation for realizing what is in the present. The means of preparation that goes into the so-called future is but the preparation for realizing the present in that future.

The past, present, and the future are transonically the same thing, a threefold, interchanging oneness. Thus, Christ is ever in the present, as well as the past, and the future. It is when one realizes the Christ in the present that one is caught up, as it were, into the Christ Consciousness of one's being in God.

Inasmuch as the experience of realizing the Christ Consciousness can take place in the dream state, it is as a thief in the night in that sense. That is, one may or may not be conscious of having had the experience.

Thus, neither the individual nor the world at large can be conscious of something that it has not been prepared to experience in consciousness. Accordingly, the coming of the Lord is as a thief in the night to the unawakened consciousness.

It is the ones who experience the Christ Consciousness consciously that are resurrected from the death of the dual mind. Those who have not prepared to receive the Lord as the Lord is are taken out only to be placed back into the worlds of duality, which is referred to as the second death.

If the reality of these things are becoming impressed upon one as being inevitable, one can reflect back on history, and come to realize that these things have been taking place within one's being in God.

That is, the entire world, one way or the other, has been exposed to the possibility of the coming of the Lord to judge the world in righteousness.

The judgment of the Lord is righteous, in that it is exacting as the law, of cause and effect. Thus, the judgment is as a thief in the night to the one unaware of the nature of the law of cause and effect.

That is, if one is unaware of the relationship of cause and effect, the judgment can take place without one knowing it has taken place; for one participates in the judgment of oneself when confronted with the living Christ Consciousness, and reacting to that Consciousness.

That is, the judgment of the Christ is the judgment of the Christ from within your being, for that is where the Christ dwells

CHAPTER FIFTEEN

Strangers in the World 2

The worlds of duality are where one receives the necessary training in order to overcome death, and be lifted out of the dual consciousness into the threefold Christ Consciousness.

The worlds of duality are not one's true home, for they are temporary worlds. Thus, one is considered as a stranger, a pilgrim, a temporary inhabitant of the worlds of duality, for it is in the solar consciousness of the Christ of the neutronic core of being that one is no longer a stranger dwelling in a temporary world.

It is the way through the core of being, the narrow way, the Christ Consciousness that expands into the universality of being. It is from within the Christ Consciousness that one is transonically linked to all things within and without the creation of God.

It is the Christ Consciousness that transonically links universality with individuality. Therefore, the worlds of duality are included within the Christ Consciousness, in that duality is reconciled and raised into the universal Christ Consciousness.

That is, the kingdoms of the worlds of duality give way to the everlasting Kingdom of the Christ of God. When the individual overcomes the worlds of duality within itself, it transforms the world of duality into the world of the threefold Christ Consciousness.

Accordingly, the overcoming of the worlds of duality is an individual, as well as a universal thing. Thus, until one has realized the

Christ Consciousness within one's being, one needs to prepare for the revelation within one's consciousness.

Thus, if one has passed up an opportunity at one time, one need not do so at another, for the opportunity-even though it may appear, at times, to be hidden-is still there for all who can become aware of it; for the message of the universal Christ is the message that is ever at the door, the core of your being, for the Christ within you is the door into the Consciousness of God.

Thus, if one is not prepared to be lifted into the Christ Consciousness when another is, one needs to continue the preparation that allows one to consciously enter the Christ Consciousness, which is hidden at the core of one's being in God.

It is through the Christ Consciousness that one is presented spotless before God. That is, by the time one has realized the Christ Consciousness, one has reconciled the opposites within oneself, and that is what purifies one before God, who cannot behold evil.

However, once one realizes that the reconciliation is the means of purification, one can appreciate the training one receives in the worlds of duality.

That is, by experiencing the sufferings brought on by the trial-and-error method of the dual mind, one eventually realizes that the way of the dual mind is the way that seems right, but is the way of death.

Thus, one consciously experiences the conflicts within the worlds of duality, and that is the purification process. It is when the dual mind has served its purpose that one reaches out for that which is beyond the dual mind.

One always has the option of reconciling the opposites within oneself. It is just that one feels no need to do so until the lessons are learned. Besides, there is a boundary, a gulf fixed, as it were, between the dual mind and the Christ Consciousness. To cross that boundary, one must do so by means of the reconciliation of the opposites within one's being.

We can now see that the purification process began at the first manifestation of the living Christ Consciousness. We can also now see that the second manifestation is the speeding up of the process in order for the world to avoid the self-destruction of itself.

That is, there is a shortening of the days, as it were, so that the destruction of the world need not take place.

It is the speeding up of the law of cause and effect that is the means of the shortening of the days of the closing cycle.

It is the reconciliation of all seeming opposites through the Christ unto God that is the speeding up process of purification, of balancing the mind and overcoming the conflict of duality.

Thus, as one can realize that the reconciliation of opposites is the purification process, one can speed up the process in order to be lifted into the Christ Consciousness.

Accordingly, by realizing what it is that brings about the purification, one has narrowed the problem to where one can deal with it more readily.

Therefore, even though one may not as yet know how to go about reconciling the opposites within one's being, one can ask the Lord within to reveal that to one, for if one has the awareness that the reconciliation is the way of the Christ, one is open to receive the answer from within one's Christ Self.

One can come back to the way of the Christ Self, and realize that one way realize that the way to find life is to lose it, for that is the process of the reconciliation that brings about the purification.

One can look back now and realize that the world rejected the way of the Christ, and substituted its own way, the way of duality. We can see that the world, if not, should have learned through experience that the way of rejecting the way of the reconciliation is not the way into the everlasting Kingdom.

The new message of the Christ is just the old message presented as a reminder that the old message went unrecognized by the world at large.

However, even though the message went unrecognized, the purification process went into effect. If one can get from the new message the realization that the old message went unrecognized, one can realize the old message in the new and vice versa; and see the message as it is, and see the Christ as the Christ is, the same today, yesterday, and forever.

Although all things come under the reconciliation of all things through the living Christ unto God, there are some things that seem to hinder the most.

That is, such things as lust, anger, greed, attachment, and vanity need to be dealt with, for if one can eliminate them, the rest will follow.

The above five passions can be eliminated if one realizes that the neutronic core of being is a neutralizer of all that is unlike the Self of the Christ Consciousness. We can neutralize lust by reconciling it with chastity, for what is left after the neutralization and reconciliation is the Transonic purification., which is beyond description as to what it is. Thus, chastity is found by losing it, not by trying to separate it from lust.

Likewise, by reconciling anger with forgiveness, we eliminate anger by neutralizing it by means of the reconciliation. Anger has no reality except what one gives it, and one has the power to eliminate it from one's mind.

Accordingly, by reconciling greed with contentment, we neutralize or eliminate greed from our consciousness. By reconciling attachment with detachment, we neutralize the bondage of attachment, and eliminate it by means of the reconciliation.

By reconciling vanity with humility, we neutralize vanity; and such is the nature of the reconciliation of all things through Christ unto God.

The reconciliation is, therefore, the means of purifying oneself for to lifted out of the worlds of duality, and of being presented spotless before the God of one's being, the All in All.

CHAPTER SIXTEEN

Inner World Travel

When one will have realized that the one world without end begins without beginning, and ends without ending, and that it is one in many and many in one, then one will have realized the nature of a Transonic thing.

Thus, to see the one thing in all things, and all things in the one thing is to see that all things are transonically one in many and many in one.

Once we realize that the Being of God is without beginning or end, we learn to live, move or travel within the context of that realization.

By reconciling all things through the living Christ unto God, one has the veil taken away, as it were, and sees the beginningless and endless nature of one's being in God. Thus, to see the Transonic immortality of a thing is to see it as it is in Transonic reality.

To see the Transonic immortality of the living Christ is to see the Transonic immortality of one's being in God, for to see the living Christ as is in Transonic reality is to realize that one is that Transonic reality.

Inasmuch as the living Christ is what you are in Transonic reality, whether realized or not, to go against the living Christ is to go against yourself whether you realize it or not, for the living Christ is the Self of selves, the one in many and the many in one.

Thus, to see the living Christ as is in Transonic reality is to see the individual Christ in the universal, and vice versa, for the Christ is not something separate from you.

One becomes like unto what one thinks the Christ might be until one transcends being, itself, for the Christ transcends Itself. That is, just as the living Christ transcends Itself to be as you, you transcend yourself to be as the living Christ.

Accordingly, each individual in the universal Christ transcends itself without doing it, for the living Christ is transcendent, yet immanent, within and without Itself.

Thus, to see the living Christ as is, is to see what the coming of Christ might be, the coming in judgment, or the coming of the Bridegroom for the Bride?

As the living Christ is what you are, the judgment is the result of your reaction to the living Christ of your being in God. Likewise, your being caught up to meet the Bridegroom is the result of your reaction to the living Christ, who is the living Bridegroom of the Bride of your being in God.

As nothing is what it appears to be, being caught up to meet the Lord in the air is not what it appears to be. Thus, the one that has ears to, hear, yet hears not, and has eyes to see, yet sees not, does not know that such an event has taken place, which is due the lack of watchfulness and preparation of consciousness to realize what it might be.

The Bridegroom is such that It is not what It might appear to be. Therefore, the Bridegroom is neither male nor female, except as to appearance.

That is, the Bridegroom is individual, yet universal. Therefore, the Bridegroom can come to anyone anywhere when such a one is ready for that encounter.

Although the Bridegroom and the Bride appear as male or female on the physical plane of being, both the Bride and Bridegroom can appear as either male or female on the inner planes of being.

Thus, on the inner planes of being beyond the realms of duality, the Bridegroom may appear as either the Bride or the Bridegroom, for the Bride and the Bridegroom are transonically the same thing.

By reconciling the opposites of one's being through the core of being unto God, one comes to realize that the Bride and the Bridegroom are parts of one's being in God.

To realize that one is neither male nor female, except as to appearance, one realizes the Self at the core of being, which is Self-realization.

As the living Christ has transcended Self-realization to be as you are, Self-realization is not the end of the journey to God; for one must continue on until one realizes that there is no end to the journey, for the journey is as the Christ, who is without beginning or end, except as to appearance.

Self-realization is the realization that one is an individual manifestation of the universal Christ. Inasmuch as the universal Christ Self includes every individual in the Christ Consciousness, the individual Christ cannot, in Transonic reality, be separated from the universal Christ.

The living Christ of God can relate to all individuals, for the living Christ of God has reconciled the individual with the universal, and vice versa.

The universal living Christ is an individual within an individual to Transonic infinity; and is, therefore, the individual Christ within you and all things. Thus, each individual Christ Self is like unto any other individual Christ Self.

Therefore, each individual Christ Self comes to realize that It is also the universal Christ Self. Thus, the individual and the universal living Christ Consciousness are transonically the same thing, which is to say that neither are what they appear to be.

As the individual Christ awareness is Self-realization, the universal Christ awareness is God realization; however, neither is the end of the journey, for both appear to be an end to something.

That is, God realization is not what it might appear to be, for what God is transcends what God might appear to be, without transcending that appearance. God cannot be something there to the exclusion of something here, for that which is the All in All is as much here as there.

Accordingly, one must transcend, without doing it, individual Self-realization in order to realize the Transonic God realization. To realize that which is in Transonic reality, one must transcend what might appear as God, and reconcile the universal and the individual parts of being unto the God that includes both without including either.

As nothing is what it appears to be, except as to appearances, one must give up everything in order to realize what it is that transcends without transcending, the Transonic reality.

Accordingly, the journey is not ended until all is given up, returned to God, and one comes to be, yet not to be. However, the journey is not ended there. It is just that one comes to realize that the journey never began in the first place. That is, the journey begins without beginning; and, therefore, ends without ending.

By reconciling all the seeming opposites of one's being, one incorporates them into one's overall Christ Consciousness. Thus, one goes beyond both the beginning and the end of all things without going beyond either the end or the beginning.

By reconciling all things with no-things, one is free of all things, in that all things and no-things are realized to be the same things. One becomes free of being, itself, for one realizes that being and nonbeing are transonically the same thing.

As words, themselves, cannot communicate what one is not ready to receive, one can become a part of the communication by transonically surrendering to the living Christ of God.

That is, if you neither accept nor reject this communication, you are putting yourself in the orbit, so to speak, for the living Christ to come to you and take you out of the body and into the inner worlds so that you can experience these things. And then after you are brought back to the body, the written communication will take on a new meaning to you, for your experience will confirm it.

The End

THE TRANSONIFIER

*Exercises in Transonic
Reconciliation*

CHAPTER ONE

The all in all of being transcends the description of what that might be. The whole represents the part and the part represents the whole.

All things reduce themselves to an explanation that explains without explaining.

That which cannot be explained, contains both the end and the beginning of all things.

As opposites are reconciled through the neutronic core of being, the explanation becomes transonic.

The transonic explanation of things comprises the electronic, protonic, and neutronic consideration of things.

The protonic, electronic, and neutronic parts of being are three parts of one thing, which is transonic.

The protonic, electronic, and neutronic parts interchange with one another. Thus, the threefold interchange is really the transonic Self interacting upon Itself.

Protonic, electronic, and neutronic parts of things have the appearance of reality to serve the purpose of what is actually transonic.

It is just that what has the appearance of reality also has what appears as an illusion in it, which is the means of escaping any one appearance of reality.

Accordingly, so-called positive reality is a bondage until it is reconciled with its complement, the so-called illusion.

Words cannot describe what a transonic thing is, for It has no opposite, yet, It includes without including, all so-called opposites.

One cannot imagine a thing that has no opposite, for such an imagination would be but an appearance.

The point we need to make is that, as it is said, there is neither male nor female, positive nor negative.

However, on the other hand, there is no such thing as there not being male nor female, positive nor negative.

In other words, there is male and female, positive and negative without there being so. It's the reconciliation of the two concepts that reveals what's there.

What appears as real on one plane of being appears as the reverse on another plane of being.

It is that so-called positive and negative interchange that allows for the expansion of the Kingdom of God within.

So-called life and death is but the transonic Self-interchanging within Itself. The one is as the other,

Thus, so-called positive freedom is a form of bondage for positive freedom is in conflict with a part of itself.

It is the Truth that reconciles the three parts of being unto one that is the Truth that sets one free.

Accordingly, one must lose freedom in order to find it, just as one must lose life in order to find it.

Thus, the mind has the potential of being a perpetual opposite Reconciler.

Accordingly, the potential of what the mind can be is but a transonic part of the accomplishment of that.

That is, the potential and the accomplishment are not two unrelated things, but a function of the one transonic thing.

The infinite mind works within the finite mind, for it is not something separate from it.

Neither the infinite nor the finite mind can be what either appear to be, for such is but the part and whole of what is, which is beyond explanation without being beyond it. That is, what cannot be described is a part of what can be, and vice versa.

Once we realize that all things are transonic, which is the reconciliation of the protonic, electronic, and neutronic parts of things, including one's being, we can function transonically within the consciousness that transcends itself without doing it.

It is not that anything changes, for one is already doing that whether one knows it or not.

It's a matter of reconciling all parts of consciousness and realizing what is there, of becoming aware of unawareness, and vice versa.

As any part of a so-called atom can function as any other part, each part is the part and the whole of itself to transonic infinity.

What is has always been that way, and always will be. Thus, opposites have always been reconciled transonically, and one is unaware of that; for there is the unawareness factor in awareness.

For example, life and death are reconciled opposites in that one serves the function and purpose of the other, but appear to be in conflict until reconciled consciously.

If opposites were simply reconciled, that would lead to a dead-end situation, but the transonic pattern of the universe has no dead-end, for there is no such thing as that.

So-called death is the means of moving interdimensionally and is, therefore, the means of averting any so-called dead-end situation.

It is so-called death that gives life its appearance of reality, and vice versa.

The so-called absolute can be found only in the relative, and vice versa, for the one is hidden in the other transonically.

The hidden treasure is found in that it only appears to be hidden in the first place.

The rest of part one is an exercise in transonic understanding. There is some repetition except for the differing opposites presented. As you will see, any set of opposites would fit into this exercise.

Adversity and happiness transonically reconciled bring their seemingly hidden sides to the Light of consciousness.

Freedom and captivity appear to be separate things, but they transonically transcend what they appear to be.

Clemency and severity are a part of the neutronic whole; yet the whole is also a part of the overall nature of what it is. Thus, the part and the whole are transonically the same thing, which is to say that they interchange with one another, thereby multiply themselves to transonic infinity.

Kindness and cruelty have hidden in them the neutronic factor, which makes the three a transonic oneness.

Bliss and misery are transonically reversible aspects of the same thing.

Certainty and doubt exist as one in the other, which is to say they exist without existing, for existence and nonexistence are transonically the same thing.

Coherence an incoherence include and exclude at the same time without doing either, which is to say the possible and impossible are transonically the same thing.

Life and death function interchangeably as one thing, just as going there reverses or interchanges to coming here.

Sight and blindness are a part of the neutronic whole; yet the whole is also a part of the overall nature of what it is. Thus, the part and the whole are transonically the same thing, which is to say that they interchange with one another, thereby multiply themselves to transonic infinity.

Strength and weakness have hidden in them the neutronic factor, which makes the three a transonic oneness.

Good and evil are transonically reversible aspects of the same thing.

Above and below exist as one in the other, which is to say they exist without existing, for existence and nonexistence are transonically the same thing.

Freedom and bondage include and exclude at the same time without doing either, which is to say the possible and impossible are transonically the same thing.

Enlightenment and confusion function interchangeably as one thing, just as going there reverses or interchanges to coming here.

CHAPTER TWO

To Transonify a thing is to realize what it is, which transcends what it appears to be.

Things that appear to be have a reality. It is just that the reality contains an illusion that gives it that reality.

To take away the illusion is to take away the reality, and vice versa.

Illusion and reality are transonic parts of the same thing. Transonic reality includes without including both so-called reality and its illusion.

One becomes like unto the Lord by realizing the transonic nature of the Lord, for the Lord is ever transonically like unto you, awaiting your realization of that transonic fact.

Accordingly, to see the Lord as the Lord is, is to see yourself as you are, not simply as you appear to be.

It would appear that to become like unto the Lord would be to become what one is not.

However, on the one hand, one is what one is not; and, on the other hand, what is not is only an appearance, for it is also what one is.

Thus, what is not and what is are transonically the same thing. Everything is transonically linked to everything else.

Things are transonically linked in that nothing can come together or apart in transonic reality.

Things appear as together or separated because of the inability of the mind to see what is there in transonic reality.

That is, the dual mind doesn't see the separateness in so-called solid matter; conversely, the dual mind does not see the solidity of inner space.

Accordingly, what appears as solid from one frame of reference can appear as spirit or matter from another set of references.

On the inner planes of being, there is that which appears as solid matter. Yet, there's situations where one moves through that seeming matter.

Thus, spirit and matter are transonically interchangeable things in that the one can perform the function of the other.

That is, when one goes from a world of matter to a world of spirit, the situation reverses itself transonically, and the spirit world has what appears as matter; and one may well consider the spirit world to be somewhere else.

Transonically speaking, there are worlds within worlds to transonic infinity; yet, it is the one transonic world interpenetrating itself to transonic Infinity.

We could say that here and there, nowhere and everywhere are transonically the same transonically omnipresent place.

It's a matter of determining how that might be, which cannot be done in that it transcends without transcending the how of things, for a transonic thing is what is, and it changes not.

An exercise in transonic Reconciliation

Become blind, as it were, in order to see; see through the single eye; see transonically.

See Immutability in mutability as a treasure no longer hidden.

See the Lord going away, yet remaining, for coming and going, here and there, heaven, and earth are transonically one.

See Abatement in intensification functioning as one in the other transcending detection.

See the infinite comprehending the finite.

See Abbreviation in expansion and see their reconciliation, for the essence thereof is without beginning or end.

Knowledge ceases that is of a passing nature. Eternal knowledge is ever being born in the mind of all.

See Abdication in commitment and know there is something eternal there transcending transonically life and death, beginning and end.

See in an infinite journey the part that is already here.

See Abeyance in operation an interaction, a multiplication to transonic infinity.

God and the creation of God are one hidden in the other; the mystery is finished transonically.

See Abhorrence in love as one in the other beyond understanding, knowing that's the way it must be in transonic reality.

See all things coming out of seeming nothing, knowing nothing to be a transonic thing.

See Ability in inability as a reality in an illusion transonically. See the reconciliation of all things as the realization of what was, is and will be.

See Abolition in establishment as a seamless combination of a threefold oneness that cannot come together or apart.

See that which cannot be seen by realizing that the invisible is a transonic part of the visible.

See Abridgment in enlargement as seeming opposites hidden in one another without being hidden; see beyond the appearance of any set of opposites.

Know that what is beyond understanding only appears to be there, for what appears to be beyond is ever a part of what is here.

See Absence in presence as interpenetrating opposites. Thus, see life and death interpenetrating one another as all seeming opposites do. See death, that appears beyond, as in life as a part of the here and now.

That is, see the transonically nonexistent aspect of death, for death has no existence apart from life, and vice versa.

See Abstinence in indulgence as neutralizing one another without doing it; see their transonification, their reconciliation unto the all in all of being, which includes and excludes all without doing either.

CHAPTER THREE

Transonic realization is the realization that transcends itself in that it cannot be described directly as to the totality of what that means.

Transonic realization is the realization of realization itself. Intellectual realization implies an end to something. In fact, any descriptive term implies something that cannot be.

Transonic realization transonically includes both so-called lessor or greater realizations of itself, for it implies neither beginning or end to anything.

Anything realizable is not transonic realization in that transonic realization cannot be directly realized, but is realized transonically, which is to say it can, yet cannot be realized.

Transonic realization allows for a realization within itself to transonic infinity.

Any description of things that does not consider the reconciliation of opposites is a one-sided description.

Opposites are ever inherent parts of the same thing. It is because opposites are inherently transonic that they can work together and apart at the same time.

That is, life and death appear to be separate, and thereby, they perform two functions at the same time.

Transonic life is transonic death, but one is not directly aware of that, for to have such awareness, one must be unwarily aware.

Thus, transonic understanding is not something one can understand, nor is one supposed to, for understanding is not found until it is lost.

Accordingly, a transonic thing is lost and found within itself to transonic infinity, for losing and finding are transonically the same thing.

Statements such as *losing life in order to find it* and of *becoming blind in order to see* contain an inner esoteric statement of the nature of one's being. And though such things are expressed openly, the message is hidden because of the nature of it.

Thus, what appears hidden to one may not appear that way to another.

The Truth of God must, of necessity, be the Truth of one's being, for Truth is transonic, and nothing can be excluded from it.

Accordingly, Truth must be experienced in that it is the part and whole of one's being. In that Truth is not what it might appear to be, one can be or experience it in accord with its nature, which is to say that one must do so transonically.

To realize the transonic Truth of one's being is to give all unto God, for transonic Truth is all-giving.

However, all-giving is all-receiving; for when one, in accord with the Truth of being, which is the Truth of God, gives all to God, God in accord with the same transonic Truth is doing the same thing, which is giving it back.

Another exercise in transonic Reconciliation
Note that you can inject other sets of opposites
at the head of the comments referring to them.

As the reconciliation of opposites is a function of the nature of one's being in God, the all in all of being, all seeming opposites come under the reconciliation of all things unto the living Christ of God.

As the all in all is all things in one thing, all opposites come under the same transonic explanation.

Friend and competitor or any other set of opposites represent a threefold, seamless, transonic oneness to transonic infinity.

To get a picture of how anything can multiply itself to transonic infinity, let a circle, which has neither beginning nor end, represent transonic infinity.

Note that any one so-called point on the circle has a center, a left, and a right side. Also note that the point is a point to transonic infinity. That is, the threefold point is one threefold point within an infinity of points.

Note also that nothing in this representation comes together or apart, and that it is a seamless, threefold oneness to transonic infinity.

Familiarity and unfamiliarity or any other set of opposites represent that seamless nature of one's being in God.

Life and death are seamless in that they come not together or apart, for they are together and apart without being either; for they are the same transonic thing.

Support and hindrance are the same transonic thing, which is to say they are that without being so.

CHAPTER FOUR

Transonification is a purification, for purification is a transonic thing. Thus, the transonic mind cannot look on evil, as it were, for it is transonified, purified through the core of being.

Thus, there is no consciousness of evil in the transonic mind, for it is, as it were, neutralized before one enters the Kingdom of the transonic mind.

The nature of the inner Kingdom of God is such that nothing defiled can enter there, for the nature of the Kingdom requires the reconciliation of so-called good and evil.

The nature of one's being is as the nature of the Kingdom. Thus, one cannot enter into the promise land of being apart from the reconciliation.

The boundaries of things in the universe are set in accord with the nature of one's being in God.

Thus, to get to where there is no defilement, one must reconcile the opposites that prevent one from getting there.

It is the defilements that are burned away, as it were, for there is no abiding permanence in such things. It's that which goes through the fire of being that becomes purified, and is that which has neither beginning nor end.

It is the neutronic factor of being that purifies the so-called opposites of being, for the neutronic factor is transonic in that it neutralizes without doing it. It's the essence of that seeming neutralization that is transonic perfection.

Transonic perfection is the nature of one's being. It's a matter of becoming aware of what that perfection is.

Perfection and imperfection are transonically neutralized through the neutronic core of being.

Thus, there are areas of consciousness where there is no consciousness of perfection or imperfection, for there, the two parts function as the same transonic thing.

Thus, when death is stripped of its negativity, it is seen to be a transonic part of life. Both life and death are transonically purified, and dwell together in transonic harmony.

Laying up treasures in heaven, as it were, is identifying with the transonic essence of one's being, which is that which cannot pass away.

Holding on to what one seems to have is to have that taken away, for such has no abiding permanence.

In the realm of the transonic mind, giving and receiving are the same transonic thing. Thus, one has, in transonic reality, what one gives, not what one seems to have.

Thus, the nature of being has what appears a contradiction; but if the contradiction were not a part of being, then being would be in part; whereas, transonic being is the part and whole of all things.

Exercise in transonic Reconciliation

Perfection and imperfection or any other set of opposites are transonically neutralized, transmuted, purified, rectified, qualified, alchemized, as it were, as they unify through the core of being; and thereby become transonified.

Fiction and nonfiction appear to be separate things, but appearance is a transonic thing, and, therefore, is a transonic part of nonappearance.

Honor and humiliation are a transonic part of the same thing, and thereby transcend the understanding of the rational mind. Thus, the perfection or the purity of God is not what that might appear to be.

Altruism and egotism are one hidden in the other, and neither can be what they might appear to be. Thus, what appears as righteousness falls short of the righteousness of God in that what appears as righteousness is an appearance; and is, therefore, a form of defilement until reconciled.

Genius and inability as opposites are what they appear to be without being what they appear to be. That is, they are what they appear to be from one frame of reference, but not from another. What appears as death from one side appears as life from another.

Creation and destruction are transonically lost and found in one another, and can represent any other set of opposites, which are of like nature. Whether it be life and death or ingenuousness and guile the one is found by losing it in the other.

CHAPTER FIVE

As the Truth of God is in accord with the nature of one's being in God, the Truth is all-comprehensive.

Truth is transonic, and not that which is contrasted with falsehood, for Truth is revealed through the reconciliation of what appears as truth and falsehood.

Truth is more or less than it appears to be, depending one one's frame of reference in viewing it.

Truth, being transonic, is what one is in transonic reality. The nature of the Truth of one's being in God is such that there is no easy way to become aware of it, for religious divisions are ever a reminder of that transonic fact.

Any religious expression has within it, through seemingly hidden, an expression of the transonic Truth of one's being.

Accordingly, to find the inherent Truth of any one religious expression is to find that to be the inherent expression of all religious expression.

Accordingly, when all things are reconciled through the core f being, the Christ Consciousness, unto God, the all in all of God is revealed to be the whole and the part of any religious expression.

The Truth of God is transonically omnipresent; and the Truth, which is of the nature of one's being in God, is contacted when one conforms to the nature of it.

Thus, religions appear to be in conflict, and must be so until the essence of their transonic nature is revealed, which allows, as it were, the wolf and the lamb of one's being to dwell together in transonic harmony.

Religion is a means of becoming aware of the nature of one's being in God, and takes on different appearances as one grows into the fullness of it.

The appearance of religion is overcome as death is overcome, but is a necessity until that is accomplished.

Religion and death are both a part of one's being. Thus, to overcome them is to overcome oneself, as it were.

Accordingly, overcoming religion or death is not doing away with them as it would appear.

That is, death is overcome when it is transonified and realized to be a transonic part of life, and religion is overcome when it is realized to be a transonic part of other religions or of what may not appear as religion.

Thus, in that transonic sense, both religion and death are there even to the overcomer, but viewed differently. That is, transonically.

As religion when considered transonically, leads to the transonically ultimate goal, which is the transonic reality of one's being in God, freedom of religion should be viewed as the inherent right of every individual.

However, one doesn't allow another freedom of religion until one realizes the transonic nature of one's own, and then one allows all to live under one's own vine tree, as it were.

Exercise in transonic Reconciliation

The transonic Truth concerning the nature of objectivity is found seemingly hidden in subjectivity.

Transonic Truth is found by losing what appears as truth, just as life is found by losing what it seems to be.

Accordingly, the Transonic Truth of generosity is found by losing what it appears to be and finding it in greed, and vice versa.

Transonic Truth is transonically hidden within itself, and is therefore incomprehensible to the dual or rational mind. Thus, the Transonic meaning of experience is not discerned by the dual mind, for experience is a transonic part of inexperience.

By seeing one opposite hidden in another, one is seeing beyond what the rational mind can see. To see one thing hidden in another is to see how there is neither male for female, positive nor negative, as it were, for the one is transonically the other.

Thus, to see things only as they appear to be is to see in part. Thus, to see Creation only as it appears to be is to deny its complement Destruction

The dual or rational minds sees in part. It is when the part is taken away that the whole is realized to be hidden in the part, and vice versa.

Thus, leader is the part and whole of itself, for it is also the part and whole of its opposite, follower, and vice versa.

The part and the whole are hidden one in the other; and are therefore transonically the same thing.

CHAPTER SIX

Becoming aware of the transonic consciousness is becoming aware of things as they are, not as they appear to be or as one would like them to be; for what one is becoming aware of is one's transonic self.

The nature of being is as the nature of God, for the creature and the Creator are as one hidden in the other.

Thus, to reach the realm of God is to do so in accord with the nature of one's being in God. Thus, one is considered a thief if one seeks to enter any other way.

It is just that the way to God that is through the core of one's being in God is the transonically universal way, for such a way is the way that has neither beginning nor end.

Accordingly, any seeming way to God is comprehended in the way through the core of one's being in God.

The transonic fact that God dwells in all, and vice versa, is ample reason to work out one's salvation in relation to that transonic fact of being.

To declare that one is separate from God may appear as a form of humility, but is the other way around since God is not, in transonic fact, separated from anyone.

It is the one who acts as though separated from God that exalts itself and is proud. While, on the other hand, the one identified with God has nothing to be proud of, for both pride and humility are transonified there.

The one who thinks he or she is separate from God thinks God is separate from him or her. Thus, one error leads to another.

However, there is relative truth in error. Thus, there is a sense where one is separated from God, for separation is a transonic thing.

Accordingly, God is linked and separated at the same time. The situation is as the atom of science in that parts come not together nor apart.

God and the creation of God are transonically linked together, and that is just the way things are, and not something to be humble or proud of, except to be both transonically.

To face the flaming fire of the Lord is to face it in accord with the nature of one's being in God. The fire of the Lord is not something one can really escape, for there is no escape from the nature of one's being in God.

The fire of being is that which reconciles opposites and presents one spotless before God.

It is the coming of the daystar into one's conscious being that reconciles or transonifies one's being.

Since the fire of the Lord is an inherent part of the nature one one's being in God, one and all must eventually face it one way or the other; that is, consciously or unconsciously. However, the escape is in facing it transonically.

Exercise in transonic Reconciliation

The infinite is a transonic part of the finite, and vice versa. The absolute is a transonic part of the relative, and vice versa.

Thus, any random opposite is a transonic counterpart of itself. Thus, sensibility is a transonic part of insensibility.

The infinite is not an end in itself, for nothing is an end in itself, for all things move in the context of the Being that is without beginning or end. Thus, constancy and randomness are one in the other without beginning or end.

The beginning and end are transonic parts of one thing. Thus, a transonic thing is an end and beginning within itself to transonic infinity.

Accordingly, contentment and misery are one in the other to transonic infinity, for they are transonically the same thing.

Opposites are seamlessly wedded together in such a way that there is no way to separate one from the other, except transonically.

There is no place where they can come together or apart, for they are both together and apart without being either.

The nature of clemency and severity is such that no matter how many times they seem to divide, they forever remain the one, for the one and the many are transonically the same thing,

CHAPTER SEVEN

Transonification is the bringing of the so-called hidden things of darkness to Light. If light were simply what it appears to be, there would be no need to bring the hidden things of darkness to Light.

Accordingly, the Light of God is not what it appears to be to the dual or rational mind.

The Light of God shines in the darkness that appears as light. Thus, there is darkness in what appears as light.

What appears as light is darkness in that light and darkness are transonically one hidden in the other.

Accordingly, angels of light are the reverse of angels of darkness, for the one is hidden in the other.

Thus, to bring immortality to Light is to bring it to the Light that does not exclude the so-called darkness.

The Light of God is not contrasted with darkness, for darkness is not what it appears to be, for it is a transonic part of light.

Thus, in the Light of God, there is no darkness, nor what appears as light, for both light and darkness are transonically transcended in realizing the Light of God.

The Light of God is not comprehended, for it is hidden in the darkness that appears as light. Thus, one must lose what appears as light in order to find the Light of God.

The transonic consciousness is ever inexpressible in that there is no rational mind terminology that can express it, for there is a seeming contradiction in the transonic consciousness, and the rational mind must lose itself before it can face the seeming contradiction in the nature of itself.

Just as the appearance of light cannot express what it is in transonic reality, what appears as righteousness cannot express the righteousness of God, for righteousness is transonic.

What appears as righteousness is in conflict with itself; and therefore, is a limited expression as to what it is in transonic reality.

God, being the all in all, transonically interpenetrates all things, including so-called light and darkness.

As the consciousness of God interpenetrates so-called light and darkness, both give way to the Light that casts no shadow.

Although we hear the expressions that there is One Lord God, and that God is the all in all, we fail to seek an understanding as to what such expressions mean.

The One Lord is One Lord in many to transonic infinity. Thus, the Lord is hidden in Itself to transonic infinity. The all in all is hidden within Itself to transonic infinity.

Thus, the One Lord does not exclude the many, and the all in all does not exclude the parts that make It the all in all, for the All and the part are transonically the same thing.

Exercise in transonic Reconciliation

Piety is transonified irreverence, and vice versa. Accordingly, continuation and obstruction are transonified as they are lost and found one in the other.

Losing proclivity or any other seeming opposite is giving it up, turning it over to God, the all in all. Then what is turned over to God is returned transonified.

Thus, proclivity is returned as a transonified counterpart of aversion.

Relationship and dissociation are one in the other a transonic repetition of themselves to transonic infinity.

Although all things are a transonic repetition of themselves, that transonic fact appears hidden from the rational mind.

Thus, if there seems to be a lot of repetition in these exercises, remember that repetition is a transonic part of one's being in God. However, remember that the repetition of one's being is transonic, and not a static thing as it would appear. A new repetition takes a new synthesis, as it were, of an earlier repetition.

Thus, everything is the same, yet nothing is the same, for sameness is a transonic thing.

Repentance is transonically the same as impenitence and vice versa, which is to say the one is the same as the other without being the same.

Thus, to become like unto the Lord in fulfillment of the scriptures is to do so transonically, for the sameness or the likeness of the Lord is transonic sameness or likeness.

CHAPTER EIGHT

Inasmuch as there are seeming opposite interpretations as to whether one should or should not participate in sex, of when and under what conditions etc., we need to bring the concept of sex into the Light of the transonic Consciousness.

To some, sex may appear as pure, and to others, it may appear as impure, and that is because both sides leave out something, which is that which transonically transcends both sides of anything.

Sex needs to be overcome just as death does, but we need to realize transonically what that means. When death is overcome, it is still there a transonic part of life. Thus, death becomes transonically purified.

Thus, transonic death is a transonic part of God, and does not exclude God.

Thus, to consider sex as something apart from God is to exclude God from something, whereas God, being all in all, cannot be excluded from anything.

Just as one must lose life, one must lose sex by giving it to God. Thus, when it is returned from God, it becomes a transonified part of God, and not simply what it might appear to be.

To exclude God from sex is to exclude a part of yourself. Sex without God is a dual mind concept of sex, and is not pure until God becomes a realized part of it in one's consciousness.

The dual mind concept of sex denies the threefold measure of the one mind.

The dual mind represents the fall from the threefold consciousness. Thus, sex or fornication is against God in that it is considered to be and participated in as something apart from God.

Thus, fornication and idolatry are not just physical considerations, for it has to do with rejecting the participation of God within one's being.

By nature of creation of one's being in God, God is a part of one's being. Thus, to expel God from one's being is to expel a part of oneself. Thus, one expels oneself from the garden or the Consciousness of God.

As there is nothing impure to the eyes of God, what appears as sex is transonically purified there.

Thus, sex as well as anything else, when turned over to God, becomes the responsibility of God. God therefore transonifies it and returns it transonified.

Accordingly, transonified sex is still there just as transonified death is still there. It is just that it takes on a dimension, as it were, that the dual or rational mind cannot grasp.

In such a dimension of sex, it is not a matter of doing or not doing, but the reconciliation of both in accord with the will of God who is then considered a part of it.

An exercise in transonic Reconciliation

The unsearchable wisdom of God, by nature of Itself, is not found through searching, for both God and the search are transonic considerations.

Flexibility and pertinacity are a transonic part of God. Thus, flexibility is found by losing it in pertinacity, and vice versa. Accordingly, all things, including God, are found only by losing, for losing and finding is a transonic part of one's being in God.

Losing what appears as God is finding God hidden in you, and vice versa. Accordingly, God has the transonic ability to lose and find Itself to transonic infinity.

Action and inaction are one in the other, and cannot be said to be simply here or there.

And for the same transonic reason, the Lord cannot be said to be simply here or there; for the Lord is a multiple of Itself, hidden in Itself to transonic infinity.

There is neither certitude nor doubt in that the one is a transonic part of the other.

Opposites appear as one or the other, hiding, as it were, the nonappearing part. Thus, if one sees obedience only, one is not seeing its counterpart, disobedience, and vice versa. To see neither, but one in the other is to see transonically.

Life goes through so-called death and comes forth as life, for life and death are transonic parts of the same thing. Tranquillity is a transonic part of petulance and so on to transonic infinity.

CHAPTER NINE

In order to get a transonic understanding of religion that is more than any one expression, we need to realize the religion of the all in all of transonic universality.

Religion is not simply what it appears to be, and until we realize that transonic fact, we are liable to become bound to a given expression of it.

To see religion apart from its transonic nature is to view it in part. The transonic nature of religion is hidden in its expression. When the outer expression of religion denies or forgets its transonic nature, it declines in its effectiveness, for in denying a part of its nature, it is denying a part of God.

Accordingly, the pattern of the universe and of the everlasting Kingdom of God is such that it can appear to split away from itself when any one expression has declined from the overall essence of what it is in relation to God, the all in all.

Thus, the religion or the Kingdom of God is that which is hidden within itself to transonic infinity.

Accordingly, any expression of religion is a transonic part of the one religion that transonically transcends Itself.

Thus, a declining religion is a part of the declining religion of God, and will eventually return to God, for it is still a transonic part of God.

Religions appear to be in conflict because of the inability of the rational mind to understand the transonic nature of them.

The religion of God is transonically universal, for it is a transonic part of one's being in God.

There is nothing that is not a transonic part of the going out and the returning to God, for the nature of one's being in God is such that one goes out and returns to oneself in God.

To exclude God from any religion or anything is to exclude a part of God from yourself.

When religion declines, it begins to assume that God is something that is optional; that is, a declining religion may assume that another can or is altogether excluding God. However, one can only appear to exclude God, and not in transonic fact. The so-called exclusion from God is ever in the foresight of God; therefore, it is a transonic part of the inclusion of God.

To appear to be apart from God does not make that the absolute condition. To be seemingly outside of God is still to be a transonic part of God, for God is both within and without Itself to transonic infinity.

The reconciliation of the wolf and the lamb of being unto the transonic, threefold consciousness represents the reconciliation of all things unto the One Religion, the One Lord God, the All in All of transonic universality.

An exercise in transonic Reconciliation

To realize the transonic consciousness of God is to realize that there need not be nor can be anything other than God.

Everything from an atom to a universe is comprehended in the Consciousness of God, for there is nothing that is not a transonic part of the mind of God.

Thus, tranquillity and petulance exist one in the other in relation to the transonic Consciousness of God, and are not things in themselves.

Everything is of God, but one must, as it were, give all to God in order to realize how all things are situated in God.

Remedy is a transonic part of sickness as receiving is a transonic part of giving.

Thus, one must give to God in order to realize what the interaction of transonic giving and receiving is.

As God is a transonic part of one's being, giving and receiving are transonic parts of one's being. Thus, the interaction of giving and receiving is an interaction within one's being in God.

The nature of piety and irreverence is controlled by the Consciousness of God, for the Consciousness of God is in control of that which appears to be uncontrolled.

As sympathy and repugnance are two sides of the same thing, control and noncontrol are but two parts of the transonic Consciousness of God.

The Consciousness of God is transonically self-regulating. Thus, control and noncontrol or sympathy and repugnance are self-regulating parts of the Consciousness of God.

CHAPTER TEN

The self-regulating nature of things is the means whereby order comes forth from disorder, for order and disorder are transonic parts of the Consciousness of God.

Thus, creation and destruction are transonic parts of that which transcends both. As out of death comes forth life, out of any seeming opposite, comes forth its transonic counterpart.

Creation and destruction are a part of the nature of one's being in God; in that sense, it's a fearful thing to fall into the hands of the living God.

That is, the nature of one's being in God encompasses both the positive and negative poles of being plus the neutronic reconciliation of the two poles.

In the process of becoming aware of the nature of one's being in God, one may lean toward the negative, the positive, or the neutronic parts of being.

It is when the three parts of being are reconciled that the transonic nature of being is revealed.

However, one is participating in the nature of being within that fourfold context whether one knows it or not, for the unconscious is a transonic part of the Consciousness of God, and of one's being in God.

Thus, one may experience destruction either protonically, electronically, neutronically, or transonically, for destruction and creation are a transonic part of one's being, and are transonically the same thing.

The nature of being is such that it moves in multiple cycles of itself; and until one reconciles the three parts of being, one is not aware of the cycles of being.

That is, one moves in the so-called cycle of birth and death in unawareness of that transonic fact until birth and death are realized to be transonic parts of the same thing.

There is no actual creation or destruction of being, for one's being in God transonically transcends both, and is not created or destroyed.

It is just that one goes through the appearance of creation and destruction in order to realize the transonic nature of being that cannot be created or destroyed.

Creation and destruction are transonic parts of that which has neither beginning nor end, and one moves in the consciousness that takes in all that.

It is not so must that the nature of being is complicated that one tends to shy away from it, for one must also adjust to the seeming fearful nature of it.

Thus, the wrath and the love of God and the wolf and the lamb of one's being in God must be faced and reconciled in order to face the transonic fact of what one is in the transonic Being of God.

An exercise in transonic Reconciliation

Immortality and mortality are the protonic and the electronic parts of one's being in God.

Purpose and purposelessness reconciled through the neutronic consciousness of being becomes a threefold transonic Oneness.

Thus, neither the protonic, electronic, or neutronic parts of being are what they appear to be.

The neutronic factor of being reconciles and purifies the protonic and electronic parts of being, and takes one out of the realm of destruction of the dual mind.

Flexibility and pertinacity are as one in the neutronic consciousness and are neither positive nor negative, but a transonic part of the neutronic consciousness.

Magnificence and squalor transonically neutralized are beyond the realm of creation and destruction in that they have gone through that in order to be there.

Thus, the neutronic consciousness is beyond creation and destruction because it has experienced both in becoming aware of Itself neutronically.

The neutronic consciousness renders opposites such as construction and devastation or creation and destruction to what they are in transonic reality.

Thus, the escape or the refuge from so-called destruction is in the neutronic consciousness, which goes right on through it and neutralizes it transonically.

CHAPTER ELEVEN

Inasmuch as the things of God are beyond what the natural, dual, or rational mind can understand, all things are beyond what the natural, dual, or rational mind can understand, for God is all in all, which does not exclude what appears to be understood.

The rational mind assumes that it can, or that it is possible to understand a subject matter because it is viewing things in part, and not as they are in transonic reality.

Accordingly, any theology, philosophy, science, or whatever that does not consider the interdimensional nature of being, and of all things, cannot determine the nature of anything as it is in the Consciousness of God.

One must consider the whole as well the part of being in order to determine the nature of being.

Thus, one must consider how all things fit into the category of that which is without beginning or end. Otherwise, one assumes that things are an end in themselves instead of something without beginning or end.

For example, one may consider happiness as something describable or something as the goal or end of something.

Although there may be states or things that may appear as or produce happiness, there is something missing in such considerations.

The so-called state of happiness is temporal in that it owes its existence to its counterpart, sadness.

Thus, happiness and sadness have the tendency to reverse themselves just as life and death have that tendency.

Happiness, as it is in transonic reality, is indescribable in that it is only revealed when it is reconciled with its counterpart, sadness.

Accordingly, when happiness it is reconciled with sadness, happiness cannot be called happiness, for that sets a limitation as to what it is in transonic reality.

Thus, happiness or anything in God is an end in itself without being an end in itself because of its transonic nature in God.

That is, the so-called end and beginning of things are transonic parts and wholes that are also parts and wholes that are without beginning or end.

As there can be no lasting satisfaction in life until death is overcome, there can be no lasting happiness until sadness is overcome.

As one must lose life in order to overcome death, life and death become lost one in the other. Thus, the overcoming of death is also the overcoming of life, for what appears as life is that so-called death in the first place, for the one is the transonic counterpart of the other.

Thus, to call something life is to call it something other than what it is in transonic reality.

Thus, no matter what happiness may reveal itself to be, one must lose what appears as happiness in order to determine what that might be.

An exercise in transonic Reconciliation

Although we cannot describe the nature of continuity or of pause, we can, by realizing they have existence in the being of God that transcends being. We know their description lies hidden in themselves as the built in secret of the universe of God.

The nature of regulation is concealed or sealed, as it were, in misdirection.

The concealment of the nature of perspicuity in dimness is a transonic part of the nature of seeming opposites.

Accordingly, to open the seal of the hidden things of darkness, as it were, or to open the secret of one's being in God, one must reconcile the hidden with the unhidden things of God.

Thus, to open the seal and finish the mystery of God, one must also close it, for the opening and the closing are transonic parts of the same thing.

Things appear to be hidden because the rational mind cannot determine how the hidden and the unhidden are transonic parts of the same thing.

Thus, when one comes to realize that benevolence is an hidden part of malevolence, and vice versa in accord with the nature of all opposites, one can see that there is nothing hidden there, for the so-called hidden part is as much in the Light as the so-called unhidden part.

Thus, possession is hidden in loss, and loss is hidden in possession. Thus, the one is no more hidden than the other, for neither are hidden in transonic fact, nor unhidden.

CHAPTER TWELVE

Without the keys to unlock the secrets of one's being in the mind of God, there is no answer or solution to the conflicts within one's being.

Without the keys of life and death, heaven and hell, their meaning is concealed one in the other, and so appear as separate and so appear in part.

Without the keys, opposites are in conflict without any end in sight, for the one reverses to the other without any awareness as to how that might be.

Thus, all things move in a context without beginning or end and without anything being aware of that transonic fact.

As ever, conflicts arise within one's members, the opposites of one's being, without one being aware of that.

Thus, where there is a two-sided debate on any subject matter, there is an unending cycle of misunderstanding of the subject matter; for neither side can possibly have the answers or the solutions that conform to the overall nature of one's being in God.

Thus, in a two-sided debate of so-called opposite views, neither side can win, even though at times, one side may appear to.

As one's being is a creation within the Being of God, the nature of being is such that one must lose in order to win, for losing and winning are transonic parts of the same thing.

Thus, both sides of such conflict must lose in order for either side to win, for the third part of the nature of being must be incorporated into the conflict.

The third part is the neutronic part of being that transonically neutralizes the conflict of opposites.

Thus, the opposites of being must become aware of themselves as self-sacrificing parts of a threefold oneness.

If the opposites of being are not reconciled with the third part, they are ever moving toward destruction without knowing what is taking place.

It is when the opposites of being become self-sacrificing that one consciously reconciles the seeming conflict within the nature of being.

There is no winning apart from losing because of the threefold nature of one's being in God.

It is because of the nature of one's threefold being in God that there is considered what is called predestination, for all things, by nature of being, move in the context of the Consciousness of God, which takes in the so-called conflicting tendencies within one's being.

Thus, unreconciled opposites have the tendency to destroy themselves because that is the nature of them; and that is what makes their destruction predictable.

Thus, what appears as unpredictable is a transonic part of what is predictable, and vice versa.

Thus, predestination and free will are transonic parts of the same thing and are not in conflict as it seems.

Things are predetermined because of their being set in the Consciousness of God. Thus, it is transonic predetermination, not what it might appear as.

That is, the transonic predetermination is not to one side or the other of a seeming conflict of opposites, for that is but a part of the overall predetermination.

Thus, when an opposite destroys itself, that is not the end of it, for it reverses to its counterpart, for it is a transonic part of that.

That is, although opposites are ever destroying themselves, their transonic predetermination is still following them through so-called death, and so on to transonic infinity.

Thus, so-called salvation and damnation are parts of the conflict of one's being, and are not absolute ends in themselves, for the predetermination of one's being in God goes beyond that twofold concept.

Accordingly, one is transonically predetermined to return to the Consciousness of God, for one, in transonic fact, cannot get out of the Consciousness of God, for nothing can be excluded from the all in all of God.

As God is all in all. all seeming change is change within the being of God. Thus, what one is in God changes not, for what one is, is ever changing into what it already is in God.

An exercise in transonic Reconciliation

The nature of assurance is predetermined in accord with its counterpart, quandary.

Equality and inequality are self-predetermined by means of their being in the Consciousness of God.

That is, so-called opposites follow the pattern set by the Consciousness of God whether one is aware of it or not.

Life is hidden in death, and vice versa, but one is not aware of that transonic fact; and so it is with the nature of all seeming opposites.

Accordingly, one is not aware that originality is a transonic part of reflection, for such awareness is beyond the threshold of awareness.

No matter how blessedness and perdition may go through destruction within one's being, the essence of what they are is still there in one's essential being.

Thus, when leading and following or any other set of opposites are reconciled through the neutronic core of being, they are still there working together as one transonic thing.

Thus, so-called opposites go through so-called destruction, for destruction is a transonic part of being in the first place.

It is the neutronic, third part of a set of opposites that preserves the essential nature of what they are in transonic reality.

It is the third part of the seeming opposites of continuation and obstruction that renders them indestructible parts of being.

CHAPTER THIRTEEN

Let us now bring to the Light of the transonic consciousness the principle of uncertainty that is a transonic part of the nature of one's being and of all things.

It is not that there is a principle of uncertainty, but that there appears to be, and we need to determine just how that is so.

As we have discovered earlier, we don't determine anything directly, for determination is a transonic part of predetermination.

Thus, the uncertainty is a part of both sides of that combination. Thus, the uncertainty is hidden in the certainty.

That is, certainty is uncertain in that it is a part of uncertainty.

It is the principle of certainty and uncertainty working together as one transonic thing that they are in conformity to the transonic pattern of the cause and effect of the universe.

Just as cause and effect are transonically the same thing, so is certainty and uncertainty.

Therefore, both cause and effect have the so-called principle of uncertainty as a transonic part of them.

What is considered real has uncertainty as a transonic part of it, for reality is a transonic part of unreality.

Uncertainty is a part of the nature of one's being, for it is a transonic part of the Consciousness of God.

The uncertainty of God is as real as the certainty of God, for they are transonically the same thing.

There is nothing that is a thing in and of itself, for all things are a transonic part of something else.

Any so-called reality has the so-called uncertainty as a part of it, which is the transonic illusion hidden in that so-called reality.

Thus, the transonic illusion doesn't take from reality anymore than it adds to it. Likewise, the transonic uncertainty does not take from certainty anymore than it adds to it.

Accordingly, certainty and uncertainty are ever within the confines of transonic predetermination, for the one cannot be separated from the other.

Certainty is a one-sided thing. So to be certain of something is to be unaware of the hidden doubt therein.

Thus, so-called certainty will reverse itself to so-called doubt if the doubt is not realized to be a transonic part of it.

Accordingly, just as so-called life can interchange and serve the purpose of death, and vice versa, faith and doubt or certainty and uncertainty are interchangeable functions of the same thing. That is, the one will revert to the other under the situation that requires it.

Thus, the one thing that takes in all things is the one thing that can perform the function of all things; and that one thing is the Transon of one's being in God, the all in all.

The indescribable Transon is that which describes without describing, which is in accord with the nature of Itself.

An exercise in transonic Reconciliation

By losing the opposites such as Remedy and Sickness one in the other, both transonically disappear, as it were, and their transonic reality is revealed.

That is, the hidden sides of both Reparation and Destruction are brought to the Light of the transonic consciousness.

With the Light interpenetrating both the Reparation and the Destruction of one's being, the whole of being is, as it were, filled with that Light.

By losing Possession in Loss and vice versa, one comes to realize they are inseparable parts of the same thing. The transonic Light that interpenetrates both parts reveals what they are beyond what they appear to be.

The distinctions between the nature of Reparation and Destruction disappear one in the other as they enter the neutronic consciousness.

Thus, one cannot face or look at the neutronic consciousness apart from the reconciliation of the opposites of being, for one cannot look directly at the Sun of being, for It is beyond the duality of doing anything directly, for the direct and the indirect are reconciled there.

By reconciling the opposites of being through the neutronic core, one becomes the threefold, neutronic consciousness. Thus, one does not look at the Sun of being anymore than one looks with It; for there, one is not looking directly at It.

Thus, one doesn't look directly at anything, for one is a part of all. To look directly at Praise or Condemnation is still to look indirectly, for therein one is only looking in part, unaware of the indirectness there.

CHAPTER FOURTEEN

In accord with the nature of being, we live, move, and have being in the being of God, for God and offspring of God are one hidden in the other as an inseparable unity of being.

Thus, in the course of understanding the Truth of being in God, you must not assume there is a separation between God and you, for one cannot understand the nature of God apart from one's nature in God, and vice versa.

Thus, the mind and the consciousness of the child of God is a transonic part of the mind and the consciousness of God, and vice versa.

To understand the Truth that is of God, we must understand that in relation to our own being in God.

However, as we understand our being in relation to the being of God, we realize it is not our being as though we possessed it as something separate from God or as God, for God does not possess Itself, and is not attached or separate from anything; but is a transonic reconciliation of attachment and detachment.

Thus, one transcends oneself in the being of God, for God transcends Itself in the being of God or Itself.

Thus, one can identify with the Consciousness of God because of the transonic possibility of doing that, for God and the child of God are transonic parts of what both are in transonic reality.

Therefore, one can come to identify with both the wrath and the love of God, for both are transonic parts of the being of God, and thus a part of the being of the child of God.

Thus, one must deal with the nature of God within one's being in God. Thus, the wrath and the love, the wolf and the lamb of one's being in God are to be reconciled within one's being in God.

One can identify with the sacrifice of God, for the sacrifice, as it is in transonic reality, is a built in part of one's being in the being of God.

Thus, one overcomes death in the nature of one's being in the being of God.

Death is a transonic part of life, and therefore a part of one's being in God.

The sacrifice is life and death sacrificing one to the other, and thereby death is overcome in that it only appeared to be there in the first place, for it is ever a transonic part of so-called life.

One can identify with the judgment of God, for it is ever a part of one's being in God. Thus, it is not that it is something outside you that judges you, even though it appears so.

Thus, the coming of the Lord in the flaming fire of the judgment on those who know not God is the Lord of one's being, a part of being one has rejected, that comes into one's being in judgment.

An exercise in transonic Reconciliation

The one thing that takes in the all of things is the one thing that takes in all things without taking in anything, for so-called nothing cannot be separated from the all in all of God, the one transonic thing.

Thus, creation is linked together with destruction in such a manner that they cannot come together or apart, which, again, represents the seamless nature of one's being in God.

The nature of creation and destruction is such that in transonic reality the one is sacrificed for the other, and is revealed as such when it is seen how the one reverses one to the other.

The nature of creation and destruction is as the nature of God in that both are beyond the description of what either might be.

The meaning of construction is hidden in devastation and vice versa. Thus, neither lend themselves to a description other than a transonic one, which includes nondescription.

Construction is hidden in devastation as God is hidden in you in such a way that it is an undetectable thing until the hidden parts of being are brought to Light.

When one sees construction and devastation as though constituted as separate things, one is rejecting the neutronic third part, for by doing so, one is rejecting the Lord, the balancing factor of one's being, which necessitates the judgment as the occasion arises.

CHAPTER FIFTEEN

The one thing that represents all things is the Lord of one's being, for the Lord is the transonic life of every being.

The one Lord of one's being is transcendent, yet immanent within everything in the creation of God.

Accordingly, the Lord is the Mediator of the opposites of one's being in God.

The Lord is the Emancipator, the Deliverer, the Liberator from the bondage of the opposites of one's being in God.

The Lord is the rejected part of the being of one who is bound in the realm of duality.

Thus, the Lord is hidden, lying dormant, as it were, in the one bound in duality, the realm of so-called birth and death.

The Lord is the rejected stone that becomes the headstone of one's being.

The Lord is the threefold reconciliation of all things within Itself. The Lord is the whole and the part of all things within the being of God.

The Lord is the capstone that completes the foundation of duality, for the foundation of duality is but a part of the one foundation of the Lord of one's being in God.

Duality represents the fall of man in that duality is a rejection of the Lord, the transonic life of that so-called duality.

The one bound to or trapped in the bondage of duality is not aware of how one got there, or that one is responsible for one's being there; therefore, one has no way of knowing that it is duality that one must be delivered from, for one is not even aware of such bondage, for it may well appear as freedom.

Thus, duality is the sin that one has fallen into. The sin is the rejecting of a part of one's being in God, the Lord of one's being.

Thus, one bound to duality does not know of having fallen into the sin of rejecting the Lord of being, for only the Lord of one's being knows that.

Just as claiming to see is denying the transonic blindness that is a transonic part of sight, denying that one has sinned is denying that one has rejected the Lord of one's being.

The denying of the Lord is unconscious in that one is not consciously aware that one is denying the Lord.

Thus, the one that becomes trapped in the realm of duality needs the Deliverer to deliver him or her from the bondage of duality.

Although the Deliverer is the Lord that is a transonic part of you, the same Lord dwelling in another awakens the Lord dwelling in you.

The one Lord represents the Lord of every individual, for the one Lord represents all, for all are transonically one in the Lord.

The Lord is the Door, the exit from duality, the Liberator from any form of bondage, religious or secular.

An exercise in transonic Reconciliation

Just as one is unaware of the transonic link between Application and Resignation, one is unaware of having fallen from the threefold balance where the Lord was a recognized part of one's being in God.

To see Calmness as a transonic part of Vehemence is to see the Lord as a transonic part of your being, for to see the part, Calmness as a transonic part of Vehemence is to see the Lord, the Mediator, the transonic link that makes them a threefold oneness.

When you can recognize the part, Obedience as a transonic part of Violation you can recognize the Lord as a transonic part of you.

To deny that Forgiveness is a transonic part of Retribution is to deny something that you know not what.

Just as there is an unawareness factor in relation to the nature of Trust and Mistrust there is an unawareness factor in the nature of one's being in God.

Thus, awareness is a transonic part of unawareness, which is to say that one can become aware that unawareness and awareness are transonically the same thing.

To become aware of the transonic linkage of Exoneration and Conviction is to become aware of what appears not to be there, which is transonic awareness.

To become aware of the connection of Exoneration and Conviction is to be aware of the one thing that takes in all things, the Lord, all in all.

CHAPTER SIXTEEN

Inasmuch as the Lord represents all things in the creation of God, and of one's being in God, the understanding of anything must bear relationship to the Lord of one's being in God.

To say the Lord is this that or the other thing is not to say what the Lord is. The Lord is not what the Lord appears to be, for to see the Lord as is, is to be like unto the Lord.

Thus, what the Lord is, is indescribable in relation to dual mind understanding. When it is said that the Lord is neither here nor there, the Lord is not restricted to being this, that, or the other thing.

When we say that the Lord is the Truth, we must realize that the Truth is in accord with what the Lord is, not as the Lord appears to be.

Thus, the Truth is neither here nor there as though someone could have a monopoly on It.

When we say that to know the Truth is to be set free, we must realize the Truth as It is in order to realize what such freedom might be, for freedom in God is not what it appears to be, for everything in the creation of God transcends its appearance transonically.

The Lord, as the Truth that sets free, is the Captor that leads captivity captive unto that freedom.

What appears as freedom is not freedom in that it may reverse to its counterpart, bondage.

Thus, one must be captured by the Lord, the Captor that has the ability to set the captives free, in order to realize what that freedom in the Lord is.

That is, the Lord frees one in accord with the nature of what the Lord is, not what It appears to be.

The freedom of the Lord is freedom from the bondage of duality, by means of the reconciliation of what appears as freedom and bondage.

Thus, the freedom of the Lord is not what appears to be, for in the Lord, freedom and bondage function as one transonic thing, not as one or the other.

The freedom of the Lord is transonic freedom in that transonic freedom is transonic bondage, and vice versa.

The transonic bondage of the Lord is greater than what appears as freedom to the dual mind.

Thus, the Lord, as the Captor of one in captivity in the universal Captor in that the Lord captures and frees those who are not even aware of that being done, for the Lord is the Captor of both the conscious and unconscious parts of one's being in God.

The Lord, representing all things, is in control of all things in that the Lord is all in all to the extent there is none else.

An exercise in transonic Reconciliation

Opposites are in bondage one to the other because bondage and freedom are transonically the same thing.

Significance and triviality are transonically the same thing, but the dual mind cannot determine how that might be.

The dual mind sees union and separation as separate things, and that produces the bondage of the dual mind.

When opposites are reconciled one through the other, they lose their appearance of being separate things, and become parts that are separate and together at the same time.

It is the reconciliation of opposites unto the Lord that produces the freedom of being in the Lord.

As delight and wrath interact by mutual consent, they are interacting as freedom and bondage as one thing.

As opposites such as concern and unconcern become sacrificing parts of the same thing, they are transonically neutralizing what appears as freedom and bondage.

Opposites such as master and slave appear as they do to the mind of duality because the mind conceives them so. Thus, opposites are not something apart from the mind that conceives them.

As one thing represents all things, and vice versa, the reconciliation of one thing is the reconciliation of all things.

Thus, to reconcile one thing unto the Lord is to reconcile all things unto the Lord, the all in all.

CHAPTER SEVENTEEN

Inasmuch as we live, move, and have being in the Consciousness of the one Lord God of which there is none else, we are ever becoming aware of what the Consciousness of God is.

Once we begin to realize that God is, indeed, the all in all, we do not exclude the possibility of realizing how it is that all things are contained in the Consciousness of God.

Thus, we come to realize there is no terminology to define what God is. However, any terminology defining the nature of God will produce a partial definition as to what the overall nature of God is in that God is all in all.

Accordingly, even an attempt to define God as unity that includes all becomes a partial definition as to what that unity might be, for the concept of unity limits the mind from conceiving what it is that makes unity what it is, for unity is but a partial concept of what God must be to be God; for God, in accord with the nature of God, must transcend what appears to be God in order to be the all in all.

Thus, to conclude that God is one or a unity that makes sense to the dual mind is to become bound to something that violates that conclusion, for such a one will assume that there are those who may be unbelievers or whatever that are not a part of that unity, and that denies the unity of God which must be included in so-called disunity to be the all in all.

To deny the God of another is to deny one's own without knowing how that might be, for as the sun shines on all, the Consciousness of God shines on all even though the dual mind is not aware of that transonic fact.

Religious conflicts are an outward show of the conflict of opposites that one is working out in the being of God.

That is, the conflict is to be overcome through the reconciliation of so-called opposites of one's being in God.

Thus, any religious conflict or any conflict of opposites that results in bondage to a partial revelation as to what God is has the potential of destroying itself because of the conflict, or it has the potential of moving in accord with the consciousness of the reconciliation of God in the everlasting Kingdom that is without beginning or end.

The Consciousness of God is a threefold oneness that transcends that oneness in that the threefold oneness is a multiple of itself to transonic infinity. Thus, all so-called cycles are contained in the one Cycle of God, the all in all.

Accordingly, differing religious conflicts are overcome when the one is seen to be transcendent and immanent in the other; wherein God is all in all and not limited in any way; for so-called limitation is a transonic part of the unlimited Consciousness of God.

Inasmuch as the conflict of opposites provides the means of overcoming death or any other such thing, it is an individual thing as to whether the conflict is reconciled and death overcome.

Thus, when one overcomes the conflict within oneself, the conflict is still there for the one that still needs that lesson.

Thus, we ever have the possibility of some being taken and some being left within any given cycle, and of many being called and few chosen,

Thus, any given cycle has the possibility within it of overcoming it. It is not until a cycle is overcome that the one Cycle of cycles is revealed and God is revealed to be the all in all.

An exercise in transonic Reconciliation

Just as Significance and Triviality may appear as conflicting opposites, and can be reconciled unto the oneness of God, so can so-called religious conflicts in the world at large.

The conflict of Host and Visitor is seen to be overcome when the one is seen to be transcendent and immanent in the other.

Just as Rejuvenation and Enervation may appear as conflicting opposites, and can be reconciled unto the oneness of God, so can so-called religious conflicts in the world at large.

The conflict of Wealth and Poverty is seen to be overcome when the one is seen to be transcendent and immanent in the other.

Just as Stamina and Weakness may appear as conflicting opposites, and can be reconciled unto the oneness of God, so can so-called religious conflicts in the world at large.

The conflict of Invariance and Variance is seen to be overcome when the one is seen to be transcendent and immanent in the other.

Just as Significance and Triviality may appear as conflicting opposites, and can be reconciled unto the oneness of God, so can so-called religious conflicts in the world at large.

The conflict of Sanction and Disapproval is seen to be overcome when the one is seen to be transcendent and immanent in the other.

CHAPTER EIGHTEEN

As the hidden things of darkness are brought to the Light of the transonic Consciousness, we can transonically understand things that transcend understanding.

Things heretofore thought impossible are come to light as heaven and earth are, as it were, joined and the infinite realized to be a transonic part of the finite.

As opposites are one in the other, they are no longer hidden to the one who sees transonically.

Thus, we see the Son in the Father, and vice versa, for the one is hidden in the other. Accordingly, neither are hidden, but only appear to be.

As the Lord is revealed to be the all in all, it is evident that every eye shall see the Lord, for the Lord is revealed to be what one is in transonic reality.

Accordingly, every knee shall bow to the Lord, for the nature of one's being in the Lord demands that, for one cannot escape what one is in the Lord, the all in all.

We can see how it is that to see the Lord as is, is to be like unto the Lord, for one is already like unto the Lord unconsciously.

Thus, the Lord is hidden in you. It is a matter of bringing the seemingly hidden nature of that to the Light of the transonic Consciousness.

We can see how it is that one ever needs reminded that the heavens do rule in the affairs of the child of God, for the inner and the outer worlds are transonic parts of the same thing.

The heavenly rule is transonic rule in that it is of the all in all. Thus, the one Ruler is the Lord dwelling in everyone.

The one Ruler takes in both the inner and the outer nature of all things. The Ruler of one's being is transcendent and immanent without being either.

Accordingly, one is forever under the heavenly rule, for it is so whether one is being ruled consciously or unconsciously, or that which transcends both the conscious and the unconscious.

Thus, there is nowhere one can go where the Lord is not, for without beginning or end is the Lord of one's being in God.

Thus, to appear to be outside of God does not mean there is something separate from God, for the so-called outside of God is a transonic part of the inside of God.

The nature of God is such that to move away from God is a part of moving toward God, for it all takes place in the transonic being of God. Thus, the going away and the returning are transonic parts of the same thing.

An exercise in transonic Reconciliation

As rejuvenation and enervation are revealed to be one hidden in the other, no stone is left unturned in bringing the hidden things of darkness to Light, for one set of opposites represents another to transonic infinity.

The transonic wedding of the opposite veneration with its counterpart, disrespect or of any other set of opposites, represents the infio-finite wedding within one's being of all things in the being of God.

Wealth and poverty are transonically united through the center common to both, and are seen to be a threefold, seamless oneness.

The three parts of consciousness become extinct in that they become a threefold function of one. Thus, what can go through that is what is, the Lord, the all in all.

As stamina and weakness are revealed to be one hidden in the other, no stone is left unturned in bringing the hidden things of darkness to Light, for one set of opposites represents another to transonic infinity.

The transonic wedding of the opposite sameness with its counterpart, difference or of any other set of opposites, represents the infio-finite wedding within one's being of all things in the being of God.

Rejuvenation and enervation are transonically united through the center common to both, and are seen to be a threefold, seamless oneness.

The three parts of consciousness become extinct in that they become a threefold function of one. Thus, what can go through that is what is, the Lord, the all in all.

The end

Printed in the United States
By Bookmasters